The Best Stories from Guideposts

The Best Stories from Guideposts®

Inspiring accounts of
God's miraculous intervention
in people's lives

Tyndale House Publishers, Inc.
Wheaton, Illinois

Library of Congress Catalog Card Number 87-50842
ISBN 0-8423-0340-5

Printed in the United States of America

99 98 97 96

15 14 13 12

CONTENTS

ONE

I Knew God Was Watching

BY ROBERTA FLETCHER
WEST PALM BEACH, FLORIDA

The long night began for me the moment I entered the kitchen. A night of terror. But all the while . . .

On the night of August 19, 1980, a friend had dropped me off at home at 9:30 from my job at J. C. Penney in the shopping mall. A widow, I live in a little house connected to my son's place on the edge of West Palm Beach.

Just as my friend left, up drove my son's wife, Bonnie, who had been to a meeting at church. She had my little grandson and granddaughter with her.

Together we went to the house, and my son Robert met us at the door. He looked so strange, so pale. Behind him stood a young man about Robert's age, thirty-five. He was the most awful-looking person: long, dirty blond hair, a black eye, unshaven, in filthy clothes. He stank from sweat and whiskey.

I thought that since my son teaches at our local Christian school and had done some counseling work, the church probably had sent this man to Robert for help. Bonnie took the children upstairs to put them to bed. I went on to my little house in back, not knowing that we all were about to begin the most terrifying night of our lives.

I had bought some little shirts for the children and wanted to show them to Robert and Bonnie, so I went back to their house thinking that by this time the stranger had left.

As I walked into the kitchen, I saw my son collapsed at the table with Bonnie behind him crying and wringing her hands. The evil-looking man stood over them in a menacing way. Seeing me, he snarled, "You sit down and keep quiet!"

"Who are you to tell me what to do in my son's house?" I said to him angrily.

Robert lifted his head and in a weak voice said, "Mom, please do as he says. I don't want anybody else hurt."

For a moment I trembled in fear—but only for a moment. Then a strength that I know came only from God filled me.

"Young man," I said, staring into the stranger's bloodshot eyes, "I hope you know what you're doing. We are born-again Christians here and nothing happens in this house that God isn't watching."

He glared at me. "Sit down and shut up!" Then he turned to Robert. "Pull up your shirt and let them see."

My son, wincing, lifted his shirt. I gasped. His back was bleeding from many deep stab wounds.

Then I learned what had happened. While Robert was home alone earlier in the evening, this man, who had just been released from prison, slipped into the house by cutting out a piece of door screen and flipping back the latch. He then jumped my son, and as Robert fought back, the man plunged a knife several times into his back and beat him on the head until he was unconscious. When Robert revived, the man had him change his bloody shirt.

"Who's going to work tomorrow?" the stranger asked us now. "And who's going to miss you if you don't?"

My heart sank; he was intending to *stay,* to keep us hostage! I shuddered at the thought of what this angry man might do to us.

Then I felt angry again, a holy anger, I believe, because I knew God doesn't like people hurting others. And since I knew he was watching, I felt an inner calm. I knew God would help us.

But things only got worse.

"Now we're all going upstairs," the man ordered, brandishing the knife. In the master bedroom he forced Bonnie to tie Robert up with neckties he grabbed from the closet. Then he ordered Bonnie to take off her clothes.

"No!" I cried.

He swung at me with the knife. "You tie her up."

Desperately praying, I bound Bonnie's legs together as tightly as I could. All the while I could see Robert's and Bonnie's lips moving in prayer.

Then the man shoved me into the closet and locked the door.

"Oh, Lord," I prayed in the blackness, "tell us what to do."

Then it was just as if the Lord spoke to me. *Help him get out of the house.*

So, with all my might, I began to beat on the door with my fist. I heard footsteps approaching. "What do you want?" the man asked impatiently.

"Listen," I said, "you want to get away, right? Go somewhere? Come on then, I'll help you." I kept thinking of all the things someone like him would want to hear.

"Come on," I urged, in a calm serious voice. "We'll take all the money in the house. Then I'll drive you anywhere you want to go."

He was quiet for a moment. I kept praying for God to let my words sink into this man's head.

"Would you really do that?" he asked.

"Sure," I said. I knew that this man couldn't really hurt me, the inner me, no matter what he did to me physically.

"OK," he said, unlocking the door. As he pulled it open, I quickly glanced at the bed and thanked God. Bonnie was still all right.

Now I was ready for the next thing God would have me do. I had to keep the man's mind on getting away. So I continued to urge him: "Come on, let's get the car and go." We went downstairs, walked out into the dark night, got into my son's car, and I started driving.

As we pulled out of the driveway, I breathed a big thank you to God for getting the man away from my family. As our tires crunched along the gravel road, he said he wanted to go to Georgia. "We'll take the Florida Turnpike," he ordered, still holding his knife. "It's fastest."

As we drove down streets leading to the Turnpike, I searched for a police car so I could blow my horn or drive over the speed limit. But the streets were deserted. Finally, we got onto the pike.

As the highway rolled toward us in the headlights, the Lord led me to start talking to this man in a natural way. "What's your name?" I asked.

"Jimmy," he answered. "Jimmy Wildner." Somehow, saying his name started him talking. He said he came from a big family of four brothers and five sisters up in Georgia. "My dad died about ten years ago," he added glumly.

He reached into his pocket and showed me his prison card. "Yeah," he said, "when I got out I grabbed a bus down here to West Palm." Seeking money, he had wandered around until he came upon our house, which is secluded in a glade of trees.

Summoning up strength for what I knew the Lord wanted me to do, I said, "Jimmy, Jesus loves you. He doesn't want you to live this kind of life."

Jimmy seemed to listen.

"Yeah," he grunted, "that's what your son tried to tell me."

So! I thought. *Robert had been witnessing to him, too.* More and more I felt that the Lord was with me. Sure, bad things had happened, but God was able to make something good come out of them. Maybe Jimmy could see some Christian love in action.

As he talked, more of the reasons for his behavior came out. "I'm the black sheep of the family," he said. "All my brothers and sisters hate me."

I told him I knew how not being loved could hurt, and then I said, "You may not believe it, but right now my son and daughter-in-law back at the house are praying for you." I knew they were.

He didn't say anything, just sat staring down the highway.

Encouraged, I pulled over to the side and stopped. Turning to him, I put my hand on his shoulder. "Jimmy, is there any reason that you can't pray with me to receive Jesus Christ as your Savior?"

He slowly shook his head. "No," he said. Then suddenly he ordered, "I'll take over the driving now." We switched and were soon speeding up the dark throughway. He kept fishing around in his pocket and complained of being out of cigarettes.

"Why don't we stop at a rest area so you can get some?" I suggested. "Besides, I have to go to the ladies' room."

"OK," he grunted. When we stopped he followed close behind me and, with his knife hidden under his shirt, waited outside the rest room door.

Inside there was just one other person, a teenager. Grabbing her shoulders, I said, "Listen to me very carefully for I must tell you something quickly." Her eyes widened as I explained what had happened. Taking a piece of paper and pen from my purse, I wrote down my son's name, address, and phone number.

"Please," I begged her, "get in touch with the West Palm Beach police. Tell them to break into the house because my children are tied up and my son's terribly hurt!"

She look frightened, but she nodded. I left the room wondering if she thought I was crazy and would forget me.

By now I was again becoming frightened. This man waiting for me outside could easily figure I was just extra baggage—a liability. He'd find it simple to kill me and kick me out into a dark ditch.

But then I deliberately turned off that fear and turned on God's strength.

However, something else began bothering me. The car. The 1979 Plymouth was Robert's only car; he had worked so hard for it and needed it in his work. I just wasn't going to let this man take that car.

It was now nearly 4:00 A.M. I had worked a full shift at Penney's and was getting very tired. I was too tense to doze so I just slouched on the passenger's side. Jimmy nudged me a couple of times, but I ignored him. He must have thought I had fallen asleep. I leaned against the door with my eyes closed and wondered, *Lord, where is all this going to end?*

As I listened to the rhythm of the humming tires against the tar strips, I kept thinking calmly, believing that God would help me out of this terrible situation. Then I silently prayed, *Lord, if this man would just get out of the car for a second, leaving the keys in it, I believe I could get away with your help.*

No sooner had I breathed this prayer than we pulled up to an unmanned tollbooth. The man reached out the open window to drop the correct change into the basket, but some of it fell to the ground. Cursing, he opened the door and got out to pick it up.

My chance! Opening my eyes, I breathed, "Thank you, Lord," as I lunged toward the wheel, threw the car into drive, and pushed the accelerator to the floor.

The man scrambled partway back into the car, slamming his foot on the brake. We both fought at the wheel with the car wildly swerving. "Stop this!" he shouted.

"No," I screamed. "Get out! Get out!"

He began slamming me with his fist, and I kept hollering and pushing him. Suddenly he was gone, just like that. He had flipped out of the car. I yanked the door shut and drove on as fast as I could until I reached the next tollbooth. I screeched to a stop, jumped out, and ran to the toll lady. I was crying so hard I couldn't talk.

She opened her door. "Come in," she exclaimed, "I know who you are! The news has been on the radio for two hours. The police are all over looking for you. I'll call them right away."

In minutes the police were there and I called home. I learned that the teenager to whom I had talked had driven on to West Palm Beach where she called the police. They rushed to our house and freed my children.

Robert was already in the hospital in intensive care with a collapsed lung from the stabbing and a concussion, but they said he would recover.

The next day the police found Jimmy in a bar in Orlando. He went back to prison, sentenced to thirty years. Thank goodness we didn't have to go to court to testify against him; the police already had enough on him.

But this isn't the end of the story. We continued to pray for Jimmy.

A year after that terrible night, a young man came to our door who worked in a prison ministry. He had a letter for us from a man who had become a Christian in the Raiford, Florida, prison.

The letter was from Jimmy Wildner. In it he said how sorry he was for all he had done and for hurting us. He told us he had become a Christian and now loved the Lord. Then he asked us to forgive him.

I held the letter to my heart knowing that we had all forgiven him already. And I know now how God made bad things turn out for good.

The Devil had gotten into Jimmy Wildner, but God had overcome the Devil through people who trusted God.

We believe God allowed Jimmy to enter our lives. When he was wandering around that night looking for a house to rob, he found the right one, in the best meaning of it all. We discovered that when the very worst thing we could think of happened, the Lord was there, just as he promised.

TWO

Trapped

BY MAVIS REHDER
CALUMET, IOWA

"The cords of death entangled me. . . ." That's the beginning of the psalm I have good reason to call "mine."

When I put a chicken in the Crockpot that September morning in 1984, it never entered my mind that I would not be home that night to eat it.

Wes and I were up before the sun, getting ready to go to another farm to help with the silage chopping and harvesting. It was a sad day for us. We had been farming since our marriage, and now, in our fifties, having failed to get the financing for a spring crop and forced to liquidate our livestock, we had to go out and work for other farmers. And what was the ironic name of the place we were heading for today? Last Chance Ranch.

At first, Wes hadn't wanted both of us to go and work there. The terrain at Last Chance was hilly and I had only driven the tractor on our flat land. But we did need the money.

We arrived at Last Chance at 6:00 A.M. A big crew had assembled already for the long day of chopping. The cornfield I was assigned to work was located on the flat top of a hill. It had a road leading up to it that was steep and winding. *That road must go up at a forty-five-degree angle,* I thought.

The hours passed quickly. I took wagonload after wagonload down the hill to the pit, dumped them there, and hauled the wagon back up the hill to be refilled. I didn't mind the trips up, but I felt uneasy about the trips down.

At four o'clock, I started the final trip down. My gas tank was almost empty and I knew there wouldn't be time to haul another load after I gassed up. My mouth started to water at the thought of that savory chicken waiting at home for our supper.

As I approached the steep downgrade, I cut back the speed and geared down as usual. But this time something was wrong. My tractor wasn't slowing down; it was speeding up. I hit the brakes as hard as I could. The back wheels skidded—then started plunging down the hill.

I tried to steer the back wheels into the loose gravel on the side of the road. Maybe this would slow me down enough so that I could ride the tractor to the bottom.

No luck. On the gravel, the tractor veered to an angle and the four-ton load behind me began to push down. My mouth went dry. The tractor gave a little leap. We were going over. *Maybe I should jump*, I thought, but too late. The tractor gave another leap and toppled over. I was pinned beneath it.

It happened so quickly that I wasn't even aware of hitting the ground. I didn't feel my face slamming into the loose gravel. I just lay there. Dazed. In shock. The motor was still running. I tried to pull myself out, but my left arm was caught under the tractor's fender.

I lay there flat on my stomach, my face pressed into the sharp gravel, my body trapped beneath the tractor's seat and fenders. The gear shift beside me had hit the ground and was snapped in half. I had just enough clearance to move my right hand between my head and the tractor seat.

Clunk. The motor shut off. Silence. Now, in the abrupt quiet, I realized that something was dripping on my leg. Why couldn't I feel it? Was it deadened in some way? I couldn't tell if the dripping liquid was hot or cold, but its dampness made me uncomfortable.

Drip, drip, drip, drip. Like a sinister clock, the sound drew my attention to the fact that the longer I lay there, the more the silage wagon and the tractor settled into the gravel, and the more I was closed in, tighter and tighter.

Panic. "Help!" I screamed. "Help! Help!" No response. I tried two long, shrill whistles that left me gasping for breath. No use. None of the other workers would ever hear me over the noise of their own tractors.

Is this it? I wondered. *Is this how I'm going to die?* Suddenly I wanted to prove that I was still alive. I started moving every limb, every finger, every toe. I felt for my pulse. I checked for bleeding. "Father," I cried out loud. "Is this it? My final day on earth?"

I'm not sure that I even expected a response. But an answer came. Birdsong. A chorus of crickets. As I lay there, I began to hear the sounds of life that I hadn't noticed before, and as I listened, I was filled with a peace that could come from God alone. Totally helpless, I was unable to do one thing to change my situation. I was absolutely dependent on God.

I knew that eventually someone would miss me. *So I'll wait for them,* I told myself. I opened myself to God's beauty. I looked up at the ocean of blue sky, at the occasional wisp of cotton-white cloud passing by, so lovely, so tranquil. God's peace and love took over my fear, my pain.

And in time I *was* missed and help came. For two and a half hours, while three different rescue attempts were tried, I continued to feel God's peace. I was even able to pass it on to my panic-stricken Wes, reassuring him that I was all right. Someone dubbed me "Mrs. Calm, Cool, and Collected," but I knew my serenity didn't come from me.

Finally a wrecker was called out from town. It lifted the tractor slowly while the men slipped wedges of wood underneath to keep it from falling back on me. When the tractor was inched up enough, I pushed myself out with my feet.

I was in the hospital for many weeks. The liquid I had felt dripping on my leg had been hot oil, which had cremated the first five layers of skin and nerves—the reason I hadn't been able to feel anything.

I underwent several surgeries and intensive physical therapy. A good part of that time I spent thinking about faith and exploring the Bible. One day I came across the psalm I now call my own: "The cords of death entangled me, the anguish of the grave came upon me; I was overcome by trouble and sorrow. Then I called on the name of the Lord: 'O Lord, save me!' The Lord is gracious and righteous; our God is full of compassion. The Lord protects the simplehearted; when I was in great need, he saved me" (116:3-6, NIV).

Today I do a lot less fretting. I rely on the peace of mind that comes from putting God in charge, knowing he will take care of Wes and me. I've been able to put our financial problems into his hands and trust our future to him.

Last Chance Ranch, indeed. For me, it provided the "best chance" to find the Source of strength to meet all our needs, great and small.

THREE

Prisoner of the Jungle

BY WILLIAM NIEHOUS

In February 1976 American businessman William Niehous was seized by Venezuelan terrorists. For three and a half years masked men held him prisoner. Here he tells the story of his captivity and reveals the secret that sustained him.

Somewhere above that canopy of leaves was blue sky, and I longed to see it. I desperately wanted to see so many things—the dear faces of my wife and three sons; my aging mother at home in Toledo, Ohio; my dad, who later died grieving over my mysterious disappearance.

I yearned to see another human face. For three years and four months the terrorists who guarded me had worn masks. The only face I had seen was my own gaunt one that stared hollow-eyed at me in a cracked mirror.

Time had lost its meaning. Countless days had blended into each other like the mass of leaves and vines that closed in around me. By now I believed that the outside world had forgotten me. My family must think me dead. What would my wife Donna do, I wondered, when in a few more years I would be declared legally deceased? I stared at the soggy calendar I maintained and noted that today was

June 29, 1979. In two weeks we would mark our silver wedding anniversary.

I thought of the February night in 1976 when I last saw Donna. It was about 8:30 in the evening and we had been in our bedroom, dressing for a Mardi Gras party. It was carnival time in Caracas and our three teenaged sons had already left the house for a high-school festival.

I had put on my shirt and slacks when I heard strange voices in our entrance foyer. I went downstairs in my stocking feet, where I found our maid trying to find out what the two uniformed men wanted. One carried an automatic rifle.

As I approached, the taller man turned and said, "Mr. Niehous? We're investigating an auto accident in which your car was involved."

My heart caught. The boys? Yet, there was something about this man that . . .

"Which car was it?" I asked.

"The white one."

I became suspicious then, because the boys had taken their mother's gray Dodge. Evidently my eyes reflected this, for the armed man leveled his gun at me and ordered me to lie face down on the floor. Two other men dashed into the foyer and on into the house.

My face was jammed into a pillow while my wrists were tied behind me. A hypodermic needle stung my shoulder. I was jerked to my feet and my eyes and mouth were taped shut. The other men rushed back. From their conversation I gathered that my wife and the maid had been bound, gagged, and left in their rooms. Hands gripped my arms, and I was hurried out into the cool night air. A car door creaked open, and I was shoved to the rear floor. The car surged forward.

My mind spun in fear and disbelief as I tried to fight an overpowering drowsiness from the hypodermic drug. When I regained consciousness, we seemed to be racing along a rural road. I could hear the car splash through rain puddles and feel it skid in mud. Cold dampness penetrated my body, and my bound arms ached. I seemed to be lying on rifles; their cold metal barrels jammed my ribs.

My captors said nothing as we sped along. As general manager of the Owens-Illinois glass company in Venezuela, I had heard of other businessmen being kidnapped in South America. I knew that there were extremes in wealth and poverty in Venezuela along with labor unrest. But in the past year we had come to feel at home in this pleasant tropical country. I kept busy with our three factories, which manufactured glass containers and other glass products. Our three sons were happy in their schools. And Donna and I enjoyed a full social life. But now everything had become a terrifying nightmare. I felt sure I would be held for ransom. Local families had paid fortunes to get loved ones back.

Finally the car stopped. "Get out," a voice ordered. Stiff and sore, I climbed out, feeling cold mud through my socks. The tape was pulled from my face. It was pitch dark, but a flashlight winked and I could see that my captors were hooded. They led me through head-high grass to a hammock, where I lay down, dazed. At last I fell into a troubled sleep.

Parrot shrieks wakened me. Dawn filtered through towering trees, and rain dripped off giant vines and leathery leaves. Blinking, I tried to make sense out of where I was.

A form materialized out of the mist and pushed a plate of beans and a tin cup of coffee at me. Then I was given an old pair of boots, and my hands were chained together.

"We walk," a man muttered. Surrounded by a half-dozen masked men carrying rifles, I stumbled into the forest, the leaders slashing at underbrush with machetes. As we penetrated deeper into the jungle, the trees loomed higher until the sun was blotted out. Hours passed and sweat soaked the shirt and slacks I had planned to wear to the Mardi Gras party the night before. At age forty-five, I wasn't used to this pace. Once, one man shouted and quickly swung his machete, severing the head of a deadly snake. My mind reeled as we pushed on into the deep gloom. At dusk, we stopped. A man pointed to a hammock in a small tent, and I collapsed into it. I dozed fitfully, worrying about Donna and the boys.

In the morning, as I picked at a serving of rice, one of the men squatted before me. "We are political revolutionaries," he said in Spanish through his mask. "We have taken you to create a problem for the government." He added that they were investigating "exploitation of workers" and that I would be released when "we have completed our objective."

"We won't kill you," he said, patting his rifle. But all I could think of was the kidnapped American businessman in another South American country whose bullet-riddled corpse was tossed onto his own driveway.

My captor took a heavy, six-foot chain, fastened one end to my ankle and the other to a tree and walked away to the other two guards who stayed nearby. I slumped to the ground in despair. How long would they keep me?

An excited chattering filled the air. I looked up to see a horde of monkeys swing through the branches. Some had babies clinging to their backs. I thought of Donna and the boys alone in a foreign country. Who would take care of them? Would I ever get to see them again?

The green gloom deepened, and suddenly it was pitch dark. Night falls quickly in the jungle. In my hammock, I lay listening to eerie wails from the forest. From a nearby water hole came the deep growling of jaguars.

Our residential neighborhood in Caracas had seemed so safe. Was any place safe in the world anymore?

Donna, Mark, David, Craig . . . are you all right?

Tears burned my face, and in the darkness I found myself praying to the only One I now felt could help. I asked him to protect my family and me. I had not prayed like this in years. Back in the United States we had attended church fairly regularly. I had served on the Board of Sessions of a Presbyterian church in New Jersey. But after transferring overseas nine years ago, we had somehow slipped away from such things.

After busy working days in the exotic cities of Madrid, Mexico City, and then Caracas, life had become a whirl of social and civic affairs.

The boys . . . if I had only spent more time with them. I gripped the edges of the hammock desperately.

Thunder rumbled and a violent rainstorm broke overhead. I waited for it to patter against the tent, but the jungle foliage was so thick that it took a long time for the drops to work their way down to my tent.

Twilight-green days blended into one another. The masked guards addressed each other by numbers. "Number four" brought my meals and spoke little. I was grateful that I had been given mosquito netting, for huge swarms of whining, voracious insects filled the muggy air; the ground teemed with fire ants and giant spiders.

Every few weeks we would move to another area of the jungle to avoid detection. My shelter varied from a small tent to a metal shack and sometimes simply a plastic sheet suspended between trees.

The days continued, droning into a maddening sameness like a Chinese water torture. Each morning was a dull awakening to a tin plate of beans, noon meant lunch, and evening, dinner. By six o'clock night would fall, and I would be back in my hammock, staring into the dark.

How long would they hold me? How much longer could I stay sane?

Easter? Could I hold on until then? The men had taken my watch, but I had been kidnapped just before Ash Wednesday. And about thirty days must have passed since then. I placed Easter before me as a goal—concentrating on surviving until then.

But the weeks went on. And when Easter Sunday came, I was still chained to a tree in the jungle. "My God!" I cried silently into the green tangle above. "Why have you left me here?"

More time crept by. April. May. June. July. In a moment of compassion, a guard said he would try to mail a letter for me. I wrote Donna, urging her to move our family back to Toledo. But as I sealed the envelope, I wondered if it would ever be delivered, and a terrible desolation filled me.

It seemed that with every rise of hope, despair would crash back in. A guard brought me newspaper clippings reporting that the terrorists had demanded $3.5 million in ransom. But the Venezuelan government prohibited negotiations, feeling it would encourage future kidnappings.

Then my world fell in on me in October 1976, eight months after I was captured. While being held temporarily in a small house, I happened to watch television. When the news came on, I found myself staring at the face of my father. The announcer was reporting his death! Had my kidnapping hastened his death? Once again I was filled with despair. I turned to God for comfort, praying for his assurance that my father was safe with him.

By Easter of 1977, a year after my abduction, my hair had grown to my shoulders and my beard looked like Rip Van Winkle's. That day my endurance seemed to crumble. I wanted to die. I pleaded with my guards to kill me, but the hooded men only shook their heads.

They continued to move me from one place to another. Since I was no longer chained, I thought of walking out into the jungle, which would be suicide. But I decided that this would be an offense against God. Slowly I was learning that he was the only One I could trust.

More and more—for what reason I did not know—I was beginning to feel that, despite everything, God did have a plan for me and would reveal it in his own time.

As time crept on, my guards brought me books and operated a shortwave radio on which I could listen to the Voice of America and the BBC.

There was little mention of me anymore on news programs. I was resigned to the fact that the world had forgotten me.

But I continued to cling to my memories; they kept hope alive, and hope kept me alive. As December 25, 1978, came—my third Christmas in captivity—I thought of how Donna and I used to shop for the boys' presents. I wondered how they looked now; boys grow fast in their teens. Tears flowed as I regretted the many opportunities to spend time with them that I had passed up because of business obligations. For the thousandth time I realized how sadly misplaced my priorities had been.

And so the months continued until now, in the fourth year of my captivity, I was in this crude mud hut, listening to the plaintive cry of a jungle bird. In two weeks it would be our wedding anniversary, and I wondered what Donna would think if she saw me. I had lost more than forty pounds, and my hair and beard were long and scraggly. I glanced down at my tattered boots, and noticed an ant on the floor. It had found a crumb from my lunch and was trying to carry it away. Long ago I had learned to keep alert by watching for any change in my environment, from the growth of cracks in the mud walls of the hut to new rust streaks on the tin roof. And now this ant. As it struggled with the crumb, I marveled at the enormous weight this insect could carry compared to its size.

Seeing that ant made me think of the tremendous resources God built into all his creatures. I thought of the strength he had given me to endure these years of loneliness, the opportunity to know him on a deeper, personal level, and the deeper appreciation I now felt for my loved ones. I discovered a kind of serenity—a kind of acceptance. I felt closer to God in my solitude than I had ever felt in my life.

As I meditated in the green jungle twilight, it occurred to me that I had just finished my fortieth month in captivity. Later, as I looked back on those forty months, someone pointed out to me the interesting parallel of my experience to the forty days and nights of rain that fell on Noah, the forty years the Children of Israel wandered in the wilderness, and the forty days our Lord Jesus spent alone in the desert preparing for his ministry.

All I could think of was that somehow God must have a purpose in all this, no matter what happened in the future. "I trust you, Lord," I murmured. "I place my life in your hands." The little ant I had been studying struggled out the door, and I realized that it was time for the afternoon news on the BBC.

What happened next is still difficult for me to believe. I heard a rustle at the hut door and glanced up. A uniformed man was standing there *without a mask.* I was stunned; it was the first human face I had seen in more than three years.

The man stepped in warily, pistol in hand. He said that he was a police officer. Over his shoulder I could see another stranger questioning my two guards, who were protesting that they were innocent farmers. Suddenly my guards started to run; the two policemen opened fire and they dropped.

I stood gaping in astonishment, confused by the unbelievable turn of events and feeling a deep sorrow for the men who were shot. The officers returned and explained that they had been in the area helping some local farmers hunt for cattle rustlers. While riding their horses deep into the jungle, they had stumbled onto the terrorists' hiding place.

Thirty-two hours later I was on a plane heading for Toledo, Ohio. Waiting there were Donna, my sons, and my mother. My hair hung to my shoulders and my stained shirt and frayed slacks smelled of the jungle. I was certainly not the neat-looking businessman my family once knew.

Since then I have thought many times about what I learned in those endless months about accepting God's will and trusting him. I know now what the Apostle Paul meant when he wrote: "I have learned, in whatever state I am, to be content. I know how to be abased, and I know how to abound; in any and all circumstances I have learned the secret of facing plenty and hunger, abundance and want. I can do all things in him who strengthens me" (Philippians 4:11-13, RSV).

Sometimes I reflect upon how I have changed. The worldly man who was kidnapped never came back. The man who came back had been given a glimpse of another world—a world within us that God wants to inhabit, if we will just let him.

FOUR

Adrift

BY SANDY FEATHERS-BARKER
KINGSPORT, TENNESSEE

How strange to find the quality that might save us in the eyes of a faithful dog.

Nothing, it seemed, could spoil that hot, windy day in June. At 10:00 A.M. my husband Joe and I pulled out of the driveway of our apartment in Gainesville, Florida, where Joe was getting his master's degree in architecture. Trailing behind our camper-truck was our sixteen-foot sailboat. We were headed for Cedar Key on Florida's Gulf coast.

"Just think, a whole afternoon of sailing," I said. Gringo, our big cinnamon-brown dog, wagged his tail. Joe whistled. It was starting so perfectly!

If anything at all threatened to mar the day it was the problem we had wrestled with for weeks. Joe would finish graduate school in a couple of months, and after that, life curled up into big question marks: Where should we settle? Which job should we take? I had worried till I was in knots. But now, as we bounced along the highway, I shoved aside my anxieties about the future. They could wait till I returned.

We arrived at the marina with the sun burning at high noon. As I stepped from the truck, a strong gust of wind squalled through the parking lot. I gazed out at the choppy blue water. A few emerald islands dotted the bay, and beyond that, the Gulf stretched to the horizon, immense and awesome. A peculiar feeling swept through me. Not really foreboding, just uneasiness.

We threw a twelve-ounce bottle of water in the boat, strapped on bright orange life jackets, and slid our sailboat into the water. "Hop on, Gringo," I called. Within minutes the three of us were careening out into the bay. I leaned over the side of our little turquoise boat to steady it against a fresh wind howling from the northeast.

Suddenly we slammed aground on a sandbar. I listened as the sand grated against the boat, hoping the centerboard wouldn't be damaged. Without that slim, three-foot stabilizer that serves as a keep we would lose practically all control.

"I'll shove us off," Joe yelled, pushing with an oar. Suddenly we broke free, Joe struggled to tack to the deeper channel waters, but something was wrong. The boat sideslipped through the blue-green swells like a car without a driver. The centerboard was obviously damaged. I wondered how badly. We were sliding sideways out of the bay! There was only one last island between us and open sea. The shoreline was shrinking to a green strip in the distance.

"Joe! We're passing the last island!"

"Don't worry. We'll make it," he said. Joe . . . always the optimist.

But around the island, the wind was even wilder. With windswept water slashing over the sides of our boat, we were being pitched from wave to wave. I grabbed for terrified Gringo. "Lord," I whispered, "I think we're going to need your help." But the gale seemed to tear the words away from my mouth.

Joe seized the anchor and threw it over. "Oh, no!" I screamed as the anchor line tore from its cleat. The rope snaked overboard and disappeared forever.

"Got to get the sails down," Joe shouted over the wind, "or we'll be blown out to sea!" In our haste we did lower them, but we knocked a fitting loose and lost the halyard that we would need to raise the sail later.

We looked at each other in horrified silence. The only way we could hoist the sail again would be to lower the hinged mast to the deck and re-rig the line from its top. And that required a calm sea and no wind at all.

In desperation, Joe fitted oars into the oarlocks and tried to row. It was hopeless. We reeled on like a toothpick in a torrent. Now the sun was sinking into a fading orange haze. Night was coming . . . darkness on the ocean. I looked back toward land. It was gone. We were lost, blown into the open sea.

Soon darkness surrounded us. Black waves crashed against the boat, showering us with cold water. I shivered in the night wind. Joe helped me wrap in the sails and we huddled in the cramped, decked-over cockpit area beneath the mast. The boat pitched so violently that we lashed ourselves down with ropes to keep from going overboard. My body pounded the hard hull of the boat till I ached.

Then seasickness struck. All night as we slid through the dark, twisted labyrinth of water, I lay in agonizing nausea. I wondered . . . was anyone, anywhere, looking for us?

As dawn filtered into a Sunday sky and the relentless wind still blew, I looked out at the most terrifying sight of my life. Water. Everywhere. Like a jagged gray blanket, it stretched on forever. "Joe, where are we?" I asked.

"We're a long way out," he said grimly. "We were blown southwest."

The sun became a white-hot laser. I licked my parched lips.

"We'll have to save our water," Joe said, as he measured out a few sips. I drank, watching Gringo lick the salt water on the boat. How long could we last on twelve ounces of water in this heat?

Hours went by. I craned my neck, searching for an airplane. Not even a sea gull flew this far out. Our boat became a tiny, floating island of hopelessness. I remembered the anxieties of yesterday. What to do after Joe finished graduate school suddenly seemed such a small, petty uncertainty.

The waves rolled by like the years of my life. Unconsciously, I laid my hand on Gringo's head. He turned his huge brown eyes up to mine. As I stared down into Gringo's eyes, something profound, yet simple, took place. I saw the look of trust. Trust that, despite everything, I was taking care of him, as always. And like an arrow, a thought came to mind: *Why shouldn't I trust God just as Gringo was trusting me?*

Across the board Joe was saying, "We're helpless. If only we could raise the sails again, but it's impossible with the wind and waves this rough."

The thought returned: *Trust*.

I spoke slowly, hesitantly. "Do you remember in the Bible when the disciples were caught in a storm on the Sea of Galilee?"

Joe looked at me strangely. "Go on."

"Jesus calmed the wind and waves for them," I said. "If he did it for the disciples, wouldn't he do it for us?"

So while the sun glowed low and golden on the ocean, we joined hands and prayed. "Please, Lord, we're trusting you to still the wind and water. Amen."

Three minutes passed. Four. Five. And then, in a moment so awesome I can still scarcely believe it, the six-foot swells melted into a sheet of still water. The wind stopped abruptly. There wasn't a ripple or a sound. Frantically we lowered the hinged mast to the deck and retrieved the line for hoisting the mainsail.

"It'll work now," Joe said, raising the mast.

Our sails slatted in the still air. "Lord," I said, "we're ready. Please give us wind to blow us back east to shore."

As if the Creator's hand were moving across the sea, a steady wind began to blow. The sun hovered on the water. We were sailing away from it, east toward land! "Praise God," I rasped.

The moon rose in front of us. Since the wind was from the west, we could run before it with no need for our useless centerboard. For twelve hours, Joe clutched the rudder and the line controlling the mainsail. We guessed we had been blown over a hundred miles out to sea. Yet, if this wind held, we could make land again.

As daylight approached, Joe neared complete exhaustion. We both collapsed in the tiny cockpit to sleep. When we awoke, the sea was a mirror of glass, the world an eerie vacuum of silence. The sails hung limp. What had happened to our east wind?

"What does it mean?" I asked. Joe shook his head. Gringo paced nervously. Fear mounted in me like a tidal wave. Was this the calm before the storm I had always heard about?

Oh, God, you've brought us this far. Why have you left us here? I thought.

Trust me, came the silent assurance.

Trust? Stranded, without land in sight, our water gone, our bodies near collapse, and maybe a storm coming. Suddenly, it seemed too much to ask.

Joe crawled into the cockpit in despair. Even Joe, the eternal optimist, knew. We had reached the end.

I stared at the sea, too desolate to cry.

"God," I whispered, "I was counting on you. . . ." I stopped, my breath suspended. For in the distance, coming over the horizon was a cross. I rubbed my eyes and looked again. It was still there. A breathtaking white cross! It seemed to be rising straight out of the water. Was I hallucinating? Seconds later a boat rose beneath the cross. It was a cross-shaped mast. Dear God! It was real! My breath came back in muffled little gasps. A dazzling white boat was plowing right at us.

"Joe," I called, hardly able to find my voice. "A boat!" Joe leaped up, his eyes incredulous. As it churned closer, Joe raised his life jacket to the top of the mast. I waved my arms wildly.

Soon, a fifty-one-foot yacht was before us. Up on deck, an astonished boy peered down at us. "What in the world are you doing way out here?" he called.

I burst into tears as a vacationing doctor and his family appeared on deck and helped us aboard. We gathered around their table below, while the doctor checked his charts.

He returned, shaking his head. "The course I set this morning on automatic pilot was eighteen miles off. An eighteen-mile deviation. I can't explain it."

But I could. There in the safe, solid cabin of the doctor's boat, it all ran together. The calming of the ocean, the sudden east wind, then its abrupt ceasing, an eighteen-mile alteration on sophisticated electronic navigation equipment—all this had made their big yacht and our little sailboat intersect exactly in the midst of endless time and water. God—powerful, ingenious, caring God—had been there through every uncertain hour. And now I knew I could trust him with *every* uncertainty, including those small, worrisome anxieties about the future still waiting for us at home.

A few hours later a storm smashed into the Gulf, twisting the sea into savage ten-foot waves. But I leaned back, enveloped in the thundering sound of the storm, at peace. My future, like the sea, rested in very good hands.

FIVE

Flash Flood

BY PRISCILLA OMAN
CASTLE ROCK, COLORADO

Why did we feel so calm when we knew there was no escape?

It had been an unusually wet June. The morning of the sixteenth, it was drizzling. But the weatherman had predicted just showers, so we had no reason to expect anything more than an ordinary rainy day.

My husband Reuben and I were driving from Denver to our home in Castle Rock, Colorado. We were still a bit somber and saddened for we had gone to Denver for my brother's funeral. Increasingly heavy rain seemed to darken our spirits even more.

Driving south on Highway 85, visibility became poor and the steady accumulation of water on the road made for slow driving. Soon we realized this was not an ordinary rainstorm. A fierce wind—now seeming almost at the intensity of a tornado—began pushing our car back and forth along the highway.

I gripped the car door as rocks washed onto the road, making things even more treacherous. It was taking all of Reuben's skill as a driver to keep from hitting the rocks, some of which were as large as washtubs.

As we crept along, the water rose and soon was up to our hubcaps. Ahead of us cars began sliding off the road one by one, ending up stuck in the sand on the shoulder of the road. Afraid of stalling, we kept going. Suddenly a huge wall of water came crashing down upon us from the hills beside the road. Reuben and I looked at each other in terror as the car was lifted up and swept backward. Turning quickly, I could see Plum Creek—usually a mild, meandering stream, but now a roaring, torrential mud flow—directly behind us.

"Reuben," I screamed above the roar of the water, "we're going into the flood!"

He clutched my hand and together we murmured a prayer as we prepared to face certain drowning. As we braced ourselves, our car came to a sudden halt. Looking back I could see we had rammed into a telephone pole only a few feet in front of the raging creek. I breathed a sigh of relief and we started to get out of the car. But the doors wouldn't open! The car had sunk so far into the sand that the doors were jammed. I gasped as I looked down—our legs were caught too, pinned in the sand that was rapidly filling the inside of the car.

Terrified and helpless Reuben and I could only sit there and let the sand pack us firmly to our waists. Meanwhile the water both outside and inside the car rose higher and higher. There was no use shouting for help—the roaring of the flood muffled everything.

As darkness set in the blackest night I had ever seen, the freezing air made Reuben and me shiver uncontrollably. With the lower parts of our bodies locked tight in the sand, the water continued to creep up to our necks. We held our heads as high as possible and tilted our noses back above the water. Although I tried to keep my lips tightly closed, I found myself swallowing some of the muddy slime.

"Oh, God," I prayed, "please help us. Please!"

Incredibly, just as all seemed lost, the water level began to drop and the noise of the flood seemed to lessen as well. A sense of calm came over us. But then another problem presented itself adding to our difficulties. In our tightly sealed prison, our oxygen was now nearly gone and the door handles were buried in wet sand. Reuben and I searched for some kind of tool to break a window, but we couldn't find anything. And time was running out for us.

In that moment of complete isolation we knew we were probably going to die. "I guess this is it," I told Reuben.

"Yes," he answered. "But we've had a good life together."

God has given us a good life, I thought. But he had always given us courage too, courage to fight and not give up. I thought of Psalm 46, a favorite of mine. It said something about courage, didn't it? I began to say it aloud from memory. "God is our refuge and strength, a very present help in trouble. Therefore will not we fear, though the earth be removed, and though the mountains be carried into the midst of the sea. . . ."

The words sounded so appropriate that I began repeating them, and as I did, I felt a Presence enter the car, a Presence that seemed once again to remove our fear.

Just seconds later a small stone shattered the windshield. Large rocks had been hitting the car all through our ordeal—fortunately for us, not breaking the glass at the peak of the flood, which would have drowned us. Now the small stone made a hole, not a big one, but large enough to give us breath and hope.

A few minutes later we heard voices. Being virtually buried alive, we couldn't tell where they were coming from. Through chattering teeth, Reuben joined me as I again recited Psalm 46. Was something about to happen?

I don't know what a guardian angel looks like, but when a man suddenly peered into our car, he surely seemed heaven-sent. Seeing our situation, the man ran for help and the next thing we knew a winch was being hooked to the front of our car. A grinding noise followed as our car top was pulled back like the lid on a can of sardines. Two men—one of them our "angel"—climbed into the car and carefully dug us out with shovels, then took us to the hospital in Englewood, Colorado.

At the hospital we were washed repeatedly, given warm blankets and hot tea. They told us that eastern Colorado had been hit by the worst flood in its history. The hospital was filled with injured people.

The next morning we awoke without any bad effects, and as soon as the road was opened we returned to Castle Rock. For a week afterward, though not ill, I went about my household duties in a sort of daze. Finally one morning I came out of it.

"Reuben," I said, "it's time for us to go and buy a new car."

He chuckled. "I was just waiting for you to wake up."

I put on my raincoat, the one I had worn in the flood. Sticking my hand into the pocket, I felt something. I pulled out a stem with two leaves and a tiny perfect white flower. How did it get there? Could that filthy flood water have washed it into my pocket? It seemed so strange.

My thoughts flashed back to that day. The telephone pole in just the right place; the huge rocks that hit our windshield without breaking it; the very small stone that broke the glass to give us needed air; the water at our nose level receding just in time; and finally that man, our "guardian angel," who came at the crucial moment.

Were those events just a long line of coincidences? I looked down at the little flower in my hand—and I knew they weren't. The events were miracles, God's miracles. He had been with us all along. He had given us strength and refuge when we needed it, and he had given us the biggest miracle of all—courage to face death itself without being afraid.

SIX

A Question of Courage

BY ROBERT R. SEARLE
OAKLAND POLICE DEPARTMENT

The woman was trapped in a burning car, and I was afraid of fire!

About 3:00 A.M. on that cold January morning in 1974, my Field Training Officer, another policeman, and I were doing paperwork in a dingy and poorly lighted bar in Oakland, California. The three of us had just captured a burglar who had broken into the bar.

I was a rookie cop fresh out of the police academy, assigned to ride with Frank, a seasoned police officer, who was my F.T.O. Frank, like many guys on the police force, was self-assured and strong-willed and appeared to be able to handle any situation that might develop. So I looked to him closely for guidance. I really enjoyed the excitement of police work, but at times I was also afraid. Maybe that is the case with rookies in any profession, but in police work a mistake can cost a life—perhaps your own.

The bar was unheated, and sitting on the bar stool next to Frank as he finished the crime report, I could see puffs of my breath. The chill of the bar stool penetrated my new uniform. I made a mental note:

Rule #1, while working winter night shifts, wear long johns. There was so much I needed to learn.

Police work throws people together in life-and-death situations, and partners have to rely on their skills and on each other implicitly. Command and authority are as important as in the army, and when there is no one to show you how, you have to act on your own. Frank was forever drilling me on the importance of self-reliance. But this left me a bit confused because, as a recently born-again Christian, I had been told to put my trust in God. I didn't know how far I could trust God and to what extent I would have to rely on my own resources. However, one thing I did know. With Frank, and in the department generally, it wasn't considered cool to talk about your faith in Jesus.

The "paddy wagon" had come and gone, taking the burglar to jail. Now all that remained after the drama of the capture and arrest was three tired cops with unfinished paperwork and one red-eyed bartender brewing a pot of coffee to keep us all awake.

I was still shivering as Frank finished the final page of the report. Suddenly there was the sound of screeching tires and a thundering crash of metal against metal, followed by another of splintering wood and glass. Frank lifted himself off the bar stool.

"Let's take a look," he said.

Outside, icy air hit my face. Down the street was a scene of wreckage and debris. A speeding truck had collided with a car and knocked it through the side of an old, single-story, wooden building. The building and the car had started to burn.

"Oh, God, what if someone is caught inside that car?" I said to myself as we ran toward the crash. In reality my instinct was to run away. I have always been terribly afraid of fire. Being trapped in flames used to be a recurring nightmare.

Frank and the other policeman were behind me now, attempting to call police and fire emergency units over their transceiver radios as they ran. Our footsteps echoed in the silent predawn street. I thanked God that the rear of the car, which was protruding from the building, was not yet on fire or the gas tank might explode. I had seen cars go off like napalm bombs. The thought sent chills down my spine. Out of nowhere, a man, silhouetted against the flames, ran toward me yelling, "Hurry, hurry, a woman is pinned in the car!"

A wave of panic, almost like a sickness, passed through me. In a few more steps I reached the car. I peered through the shattered glass of the passenger window and tried the door, but the impact had jammed it shut. The woman was pinned under the dashboard and appeared unconscious. Flames were crackling, but the fire was mostly contained under the hood and hadn't spread to the car interior. I was sweating now, despite the cold. I pushed out the rest of the broken glass with my hands, ripping my gloves.

Leaning through the passenger window I grabbed the woman's arm. Frank came running up.

"Engines are on the way," he yelled. He climbed in the backseat through the rear door on the driver's side.

"Pull her up," he yelled. I tried to lift her high enough for him to reach, but she wouldn't budge and he was unable to grasp her from the rear seat. The passerby, who had warned me, tried reaching in through the driver's window but was only able to take hold of her ankle. We struggled vainly. "Hey, the fire's spreading!" the man shouted. It was hard to hear over the crackling blaze. Frank backed out of the car.

"Get away from the car! Gas is spilling all over!" he yelled. I was trained to follow his orders, but I hesitated. The heat was intense.

"Back out! Get away from the car!" Frank yelled again.

I looked across the front seat through the smoke; the passerby was gone. Our rescue attempt had failed. I had to accept the fact. I retreated back with the others.

Safely away, I could see the flames spreading over the top of the car and up through the old building. Now the interior of the car was filling with smoke. A cold wind blew over us, wafting the oily fumes. All I could think of was the poor woman trapped in the flames. It was like my nightmare. Trapped! Burning!

"We did all we could. But she's done for," Frank said.

My heart was beating wildly. "God, I can't do a thing. Can't you save her?" I pleaded.

Then into my mind flashed a thought from Matthew 18:14—*I wish that none perish.*

"God. You aren't telling me to get back in that car, are you? Three of us just failed in our attempt to free her." My heart felt like it had stopped beating. I was terrified because I knew I had to give it another try.

"Jesus. You promised to be my strength in my weaknesses, and you know that I'm petrified of fire, so you're going to have to be the one who does it," I prayed.

Taking a deep breath, I started forward. My legs propelled me toward the burning car. *Just one more attempt.* The fire prevented entry now on the driver's side of the car. I ran around to the other side. "God, help me get this rear door open," I prayed. I sensed his nearness. My fear was still with me—but somehow it was held in check.

Praise God! The door moved enough so I could slide sideways into the backseat. Once inside, I couldn't see because of the thick smoke and my smarting eyes.

"Lord, show me! Help us get out of here!" I said out loud.

I had to move fast before the gas tank burst. Leaning over the front seat, I groped for the woman. The smoke cleared for one moment and I saw that the ends of her hair were starting to burn. I was able to reach her head and bat the fire out with my gloved hands. Larger flames started appearing through the dashboard. I was terribly off balance, stretched way over the front seat . . . impossible to lift her. My feet were slipping on broken glass lying on the floor; my hands just touched her. Not knowing how I was going to get leverage to lift her, I pleaded loudly for God's help. Bent over and stretched out, I got my hand barely under her. But when I lifted, she was much lighter than I imagined. It was as if her body was raised effortlessly.

Then I had her secure in my arms. Smoke swirled around as I tried to edge out, but we couldn't both get through the small gap in the door. I kicked with my foot but it wouldn't open any more. So I pushed her feet out through the opening. Outside the passerby ran up and grabbed her legs; he tugged and she bounced out.

Then, twisting and pushing, I slipped beneath the metal jaws of the door. I ran. Before I was twenty feet away, the car was completely engulfed in flames.

I ran over to the small circle of onlookers, panting. Eyes watering from the smoke. Praising God, we stood in silence for a moment.

"Bob, I wanted to help you, but I've been afraid of fire all my life," Frank whispered, resting his hand on my shoulder.

"So have I," I replied, looking up and inhaling a breath of fresh air.

"There's no way . . . I thought, humanly speaking, there was just no possible way we could get her out," he said.

"There wasn't," I said.

We looked at each other for a long moment—two cops, a seasoned veteran and a green rookie—and we both understood.

SEVEN

Out of Control!

BY JOSEPHINE CARTER
WHITE PLAINS, NEW YORK

It was not a radiant Easter Sunday. The sun remained hidden behind dark clouds that threatened rain. But the early-morning service in that freshly painted old New England church, with its steeple pointing majestically up toward the sky, seemed especially meaningful to me that day. The anthem, "There Is No Death," was beautiful and stirring, as was the traditional Easter message of life eternal. I left the church humming the last hymn, uplifted and glad to be alive.

A friend and I had driven to Massachusetts for the weekend, and we left shortly after the service in her four-door Mercury sedan for the long ride home. We were to pick up another friend in Rhode Island, about an hour's drive away. Immersed in our own thoughts, we drove for some time without talking, when Barbara suddenly asked, "Do you ever read the Bible, Jo? Do you understand it?"

I was rather startled at the questions so suddenly sprung at me.

Hardly any of my friends ever discussed religion, considering it very personal.

"I'm trying to understand it," I said. "Lately I've begun to read with a different attitude—an open mind, a willingness to learn from it. So much of it seems new to me, so much wisdom to grasp."

She asked, "Do you have a favorite verse?"

"Yes," I said, "in Psalms. 'God is our refuge and strength, a very present help in trouble'" (Psalm 46:1).

She nodded, agreeing. "Wouldn't it be wonderful to have such faith that, no matter what happens, you could put your trust in the Lord without any doubt of his protection?"

"Yes, it would."

In the silence that followed, I asked myself, *If put to the test, would I respond calmly, with faith and trust? Or would I panic?* I silently prayed I would know his help was present.

We talked of other things, and in a short while reached the home of our friend, Anne. I got into the backseat and we drove along for about an hour when Barbara, who was driving, said she felt sleepy. It was very warm in the car, I thought, and we all agreed we had better stop for coffee as soon as possible. I believe Barbara then opened her window a bit and said she would munch on a candy bar to keep awake.

I don't recall how many more miles we drove—probably quite a distance. I was gazing out the side window, lost in my own private thoughts, when I suddenly felt the car swerve, and as I looked to the front I saw it zigzagging across the road. The rain had come at last, and we had been driving at the maximum speed on this well-traveled highway southwest of Providence. I realized in a flash that the car was completely out of control.

Humanly, there was nothing we could do. It was too late. My first fearful thought was that this was the end. But just as quick as lightning that beautiful verse from Psalms about protection came to me so clearly, and I prayed as I had never prayed before, confident of God's "ever present" help for all of us.

All fear left me instantly. As we went through the guardrail, twisting and turning over and over down an embankment, I continued to pray. Then came a shattering impact, that awful crash that still rings in my ears. Slowly I became aware that I was still alive, wedged somewhere in the bottom of the automobile.

I felt no pain, no bruises, no bleeding, only the most comforting sensation that I was somehow enveloped in the everlasting arms of Almighty God—in his care, his love, which seemed to be beneath, around and above me, a feeling I shall never forget. I don't even recall a bump—only hearing that horrible smashing sound all around us; and there I was, in an upside-down position, unable to free myself but seemingly unhurt.

A terrifying thought gripped me. What about the others in the front seat? Could they still be alive? How could they have survived this accident?

Then I heard a weak voice that seemed to come from a million miles away. "I'm bleeding, I'm bleeding. I must get out of here!"

And another voice said softly, but painfully, "My head, my head, something heavy on my head." Then dead silence. A dreadful silence.

After what seemed an eternity, but probably not more than a minute or two, someone gently helped me out of the car. I told them I was all right, but we must get the others out.

"How many?" someone asked.

"Two others, but quick, very quick, we must hurry," I replied.

People seemed to be running toward the car from all directions. A man's voice called to someone to turn off the ignition immediately.

The sound of an ambulance siren coming nearer was frightening, and so many people standing around—just looking. Still no sound from those in the front seat of the car.

Suddenly I noticed some commotion on the other side of the car. Were they at last getting my friends out? There were too many people around that area for me to see clearly, but it appeared they were at least alive. I walked closer.

The ambulance had arrived, and someone was being put on a stretcher. I couldn't tell at first whether it was Barbara or Anne. Then I saw Anne bleeding profusely from the nose and being helped to the ambulance. Blood was splattered all over her white coat. But, thank God, they were both still alive. Before I knew it we were all in the ambulance and rushed at high speed, siren screaming, to the nearest hospital, about ten miles away.

In the ambulance I sat beside Barbara, who was on the stretcher. The upper part of her face was cut, bruised, and swollen. It was obvious she had head injuries, but it was difficult at this point to determine how serious they were. She looked up at me and murmured, "Are we all alive?"

I nodded. "Yes," I whispered, "we are. But don't try to talk now. Try to rest."

Then I heard her say, "Thank God and thank you, too, Jo," and she closed her eyes.

Why was she thanking me? I wondered.

I looked over to the far end of the ambulance where Anne was sitting. Her head was tipped backward, and an attendant was administering first aid. She didn't speak. How badly was she hurt? I wanted to take her hand and comfort her but I was too far away. I simply said, "We'll soon be at the hospital, Anne."

At the hospital, my two friends were admitted immediately to the emergency area, and I gave the lady at the receiving desk the necessary information. She wanted to give me a sedative—at least a cup of coffee. I settled for the coffee. Then I went to the ladies' room to freshen up. I washed my hands, combed my hair, and started to walk out when I turned abruptly and walked back to the mirror. Yes, it was I. What happened wasn't a dream after all but very real, and my friends might be seriously hurt.

Out in the hospital corridor, I paced the floor for awhile and then sat down. Soon a doctor appeared, and I asked about my friends. Could I see them? He told me they had taken seven or eight X rays and that both were free of any internal injuries.

"It's a miracle," he said. "You were all very lucky."

Then the doctor told us we could be released. I made arrangements for us to take the train home—about a three-hour ride—and for someone to meet us when we arrived.

On the train, Barbara found a seat for herself. I sat next to Anne. She asked me how I felt. I assured her I was just fine. She told me that neither she nor Barbara lost consciousness at any time and that Barbara had had the presence of mind to turn off the ignition herself when she heard someone yelling that the car might explode. I told her how baffled I was that we were all so quiet at the time of the accident. Not one outburst of fear from any of us.

"We just heard you praying for us, Jo," she said.

"Do you mean I was praying out loud?" I asked. I thought I had prayed silently.

"Yes, you were saying over and over again for us not to be afraid; that you knew God would take care of us—protect us. It was very helpful."

I didn't know what to say. I was embarrassed. But I was pleased to know it had helped. Was that why Barbara had said, "Thank you, too, Jo"?

I couldn't help thinking during the long ride home of how tragically this day might have ended. To others, our escape might have just seemed "lucky." But, to me, it was simply a proof of the power of God's Word.

I remember how Barbara and I had talked about the Bible and I had quoted my favorite verse. How instantly those words had come to mind when they were so desperately needed, with faith displacing fear. How true, I thought are the words, "The Lord is nigh unto all them that call upon him . . . in truth" (Psalm 145:18). I saw so clearly now that the whole day had been preparing me for what was to come, beginning with the Easter service, then my talk with Barbara, then my own prayerful thoughts. And I was ready when the time came to face a crisis.

That frightening experience actually was a blessing in disguise. From it I developed a new love for the Bible that had for so long lain on my bedside table unopened. I vowed that, for me at least, it would no longer be a closed book, for I had learned that the Bible is more than the Book of Life. It is the Gift of Life.

EIGHT

The Prayer That Brought Us Home

BY FAYE KING
AUSTIN, ARKANSAS

Held hostage by desperate men, we prayed.

Soft September rain was soaking into our good farm soil that Wednesday evening. I was sitting in my favorite recliner in the living room of our small frame home, my Bible in my lap. But the words were blurred. Across from me my husband, John, sat quietly in his green recliner, looking at one of our unexpected visitors. We had relaxed in our chairs many evenings since my husband had retired. Now I wondered if we would die in them.

Our nightmare had begun several minutes—an eternity—earlier, when my husband answered a knock on the door. A man of medium height stood there, raindrops glistening on his dark hair. His damp white T-shirt clung to his muscular body; his tight jeans were splashed with mud. His voice and his smile were warm and pleasant.

"Our truck is in the ditch; could I come in and call a wrecker?"

"Sure, come on in," my husband replied. The man entered, and my husband led him to the hall telephone. As he was thumbing through the yellow pages, another man in a black T-shirt had come to the door. Wet brown hair framed a fragile face.

"Could I use the bathroom while he uses your phone?"

Another "sure," another entry. And then, three more men were at the door. But this time, instead of smiles and polite inquiries, there were pistols and a sawed-off shotgun pushing their way into our home. A tall, blond man, his thick mustache hovering over a thin-lipped smile, pushed the barrel of the shotgun into my stomach. I backed into the far wall of the living room, my head tilted back, staring into glacier blue eyes.

"Hello, there, lady, glad to make your acquaintance." He turned his head, but the shotgun never moved an inch. "Well, Larry, big man, you say you're in charge, what's next?"

Afraid to breathe, I inched my head around to look at the slight man in the black T-shirt, now sitting on the edge of the couch, his face contorted with pain. I couldn't see my husband. "Dear God, had they taken him into another room to kill him?"

"Bring them both over here," Larry said wearily. Relief washed over me as I heard the word *both*.

My captor removed the shotgun. "Get over there to the big man, honey." I turned and walked over to the couch. Before I got there, I felt the gun barrel nestle between my shoulder blades. A fourth man, thick-bodied and dark-skinned, pushed my husband to my side.

Larry stood and slowly pulled the T-shirt almost up to his chin. "Take a good look, both of you, and listen." I gazed at a small round hole that looked as though it had been drawn with a red pen, inches above his heart. "We've escaped from a prison in Tennessee, and we've already shot one man while escaping. We won't hesitate to shoot anyone who gets in our way. Now," he continued, "we're taking over your house for the night. If you do as we say, you won't be hurt. If you don't . . ."

He pulled his shirt back down and didn't finish his sentence. He knew it wasn't necessary.

"Now, I want all three of you to sit down somewhere." Larry's voice never lost its softness. "And don't get any funny ideas about escaping. We have some things we have to do."

He had said, "all three of you." Where was the third person? Then, I realized the truth. My eyes focused on a young man, standing rigidly in front of the man who had first come to our door. When he walked to a chair I saw the reason for his stiffness—a pistol had been shoved into his back. I wondered where he had been kidnapped and what fate he would share with us.

"You heard the big man," my blond-haired guard barked, "now sit down!" He nudged me with the shotgun. I walked to my recliner and fell into its familiar softness. My husband walked slowly to his own chair. I was heartened by my husband's calmness.

From my seat in the living room, I could see a man in each of our three bedrooms, opening drawers, throwing clothing and personal items out into heaps. My mind screamed at them to stop. How dare they come into our home and throw our things about as casually as rags! Their presence had turned a love-filled home into a house loaded with their violence and hatred.

"Big man, we've checked out everything." It was the blond giant's now familiar voice.

"Listen, Dude, I've had about enough of this big man talk, see?" Larry stood up. Lamplight glinted on his gun barrel.

"Yeah, well, why don't we decide who the real man of this outfit is?" "Dude" walked over to Larry and towered above him, his pistol pointed at Larry's stomach.

"OK, why don't we?" Larry stood there, staring up at the bigger man.

I'm going to see a man die on my living room floor! I felt as though I were going to suffocate as I watched the two men staring at each other. I could see Larry's eyes, and I knew I was looking at death. He would kill the big man as casually as I would swat a fly.

The big man must have realized the same thing, because he put his gun down at his side and gave a small laugh. "Hey, man, don't get all uptight—the strain is getting to us."

One of the men turned on the television set to check on news bulletins. Another turned out all the lights except for the lamp that was now shedding a soft light on my worn Bible.

But the light was doing no good—fear and anger had blinded me. Desperately, I tried to remember the Twenty-third Psalm. *The Lord is my Shepherd . . .* , but fear was paralyzing my mind—I couldn't remember the psalm! "Dear God," I prayed, "I can't read or remember your Word, and maybe I'm going to die. Show me what to do!"

"OK, you'd better go to bed now." Larry's words interrupted my frantic thoughts. "And, remember, there's a guard at your bedroom door and it won't bother him a bit to pull the trigger if you try anything."

My husband and I were sent to the guest bedroom, the young hostage to another bedroom. One of the convicts pulled a chair to our doorway and sat with a shotgun.

In the dark bedroom, clinging to my husband, I listened to the grandfather clock chime away the hours—one o'clock, two o'clock. . . . Suddenly, I felt a compelling urge to pray—aloud—as though God were instructing me to voice my fear and concern.

But I just couldn't. Praying aloud in church was one thing—praying aloud in front of four desperate criminals was quite another! I had heard the newscaster's warning: "Remember, these men are armed and considered very dangerous."

I had looked at their taut faces. I didn't want to upset them any further. But the urging became stronger—it was as though God's gentle hands were giving me a nudge. I sat up on the bed, and the convict guarding the door straightened in his chair. My own voice startled me. "Do you mind if I pray?"

"What did she say?" I recognized Larry's voice.

"She wants to know if she can pray," our bedroom guard replied.

A long silence—then, "I guess it will be all right."

I knelt down by the bed and began pouring out my heart, and the sobs I had been holding inside began tearing out of me. I prayed for my husband and myself and the young hostage. Then I prayed for my children, asking God to give them strength, no matter what happened to us. I paused a moment, but still felt a sense of urgency. *Pray for the four men*—more gentle nudging.

Pray for kidnappers and thieves? My mind balked. *I died for kidnappers and thieves, and you.*

"And Father," my sobbing voice sounded harsh and unreal, "bless these men, bless their folks, and help them to see that you love them and will forgive them."

I don't remember what else I said, but I remember how I felt. A warm blanket of divine love began covering my fear and hatred. After I finished, I got back on the bed with my husband, and a Scripture verse softly slipped into my mind—"And, lo, I am with you always, even unto the end of the world" (Matthew 28:20). I clung to that verse until morning finally came.

"Mrs. King, we're splitting up this morning; two men are going to take your truck, and Lyons and myself are going to take your car. We're taking you and Mr. King along as hostages." Larry's voice was gruff, but not unkind.

The tall blond man got the truck keys from my husband, and he and the shorter dark-skinned man hurried out the kitchen door. As I heard the truck motor start, I looked at Larry. But this time I did not see an escaped convict. I saw a human being. *This is some mother's son,* I thought.

"Don't you want me to fix all of us some breakfast?" My voice was calm.

"No, I don't want to take the time to eat." Larry looked at me and smiled. "You know, you remind me of my grandmother." His smile faded and the hard, set look came back on his face. "Come on, let's go—and remember, Mr. King, we're watching every move you make. You do the driving and I'll ride in the front seat. Mrs. King can get in the back with Lyons." We walked out to the car.

"My arthritis bothers me when I ride in the backseat. I should ride in the front seat with my husband." (Was that my voice that had said that?)

"Well, all right, Mrs. King, get in front. But just remember, there are guns pointed at both of you."

"Where's the young boy?" I held my breath, waiting for his answer.

"He's tied and gagged—now get in this car!" Larry and Lyons got in the back, my husband and I got in the front, and the nightmare continued.

We drove through the day, carefully, avoiding all the main highways, stopping only once to get gas and use the bathroom, listening to the news bulletins all the way.

The young hostage had managed to untie himself back at our house and alert the police. Now the news bulletins were changed—"An elderly couple, Mr. and Mrs. John King, have been kidnapped. Roadblocks are being set up through the area." Later, another news flash: "Two of the kidnappers have been captured. The search continues for the Kings."

About four o'clock that afternoon, Larry instructed my husband to pull over into a wooded area so that they could plan the best route. The rain had ended and the afternoon sun was filtering through the trees. I opened my purse, took out a small book of devotions and started reading. The gentle urging began once more. . . . *Talk to them.*

"What will I say, Father?"

Talk to them from your heart.

"Why don't you boys give yourselves up?" I said. "Your mothers would rather see you in prison than dead."

"We'll die before we go back to prison," Larry said.

Lyons nodded.

I asked Larry why he was in prison, and he explained that he had started using dope while in Vietnam. After going back to a few schools he was "into dope really heavy" and started selling it, which led to his arrest. Again I urged them to turn themselves in, but suddenly our talk was interrupted by the sound of a truck motor. Larry jumped from the car and watched the truck as it pulled into the wooded area. Lyons covered him as he sauntered over to the truck, a smile on his face. He started talking to the driver, then pulled his pistol out of his pocket.

"We're taking this truck. Get out and leave the keys." His voice, so soft minutes earlier, had turned to flint.

But the driver rammed his foot on the accelerator and backed the truck out, slinging mud and gravel. With a curse, Larry ran to get our car and told my husband to move over.

"I'm going to catch up with those guys and take that truck!" He gunned the motor and pulled out like a madman, pursuing the truck down the narrow road. Another prayer bounced in my head: "Lord, you said you'd be with us. Please don't leave us now!"

We soon caught up with the truck and forced it over to the side of the highway. Larry jumped out, made the driver move over, and spun out onto the highway. Lyons instructed my husband to pull out also. Suddenly I heard a siren, and when I looked back, I saw beautiful flashing blue lights. We were going to be rescued!

But we weren't. The police car sped by us, pursuing the truck!

On and on we drove, avoiding freeways and main highways, until we came to Covington, Kentucky. Lyons instructed my husband to drive to a certain street, then leaned toward me from the backseat. "Mrs. King, do you have two dollars?"

The news bulletins had said that Lyons was wanted for armed robbery and assault with a deadly weapon. He knew we had a lot of cash with us—we had paid for everything during the trip—yet he watched me thumb through the larger bills until I found the two dollars. I handed them to him.

He looked at me a moment. "Thank you," he said softly, then opened the car door and melted into the night.

My husband and I looked at each other for a moment before reality finally dawned. The nightmare was over and we were safe. I did what I had done in my darkened bedroom earlier—cried and prayed—but this time all I said was, "Thank you, God."

After we arrived home, we learned that Larry had been captured. I copied down some of my favorite Scripture verses and mailed them to him in prison.

A few days later, a letter came from him: "Mrs. King, you'll never know how much your prayer meant to me that night we forced our way into your home. I was reared in a Christlike home, and you and Mr. King reminded me of my own parents. I went in the wrong direction when I started putting myself before God. Thank you for seeing some good in me—so many people see only the bad in others. You'll never know how much your prayer meant."

Larry was wrong about that. I do know what the prayer meant—to my own life, too. When I was totally helpless—unable to read or even remember God's Word—I still had access to him, through prayer. When I prayed for those men, I felt the compassion of Christ reaching out toward them through me. That was why, the next morning, I was able to look at them as Christ looks at all of us—past human sin to human need.

NINE

The Lifeline

BY BRUCE LARSON
SANIBEL, FLORIDA

It was invisible. Yet it was there.

Two years ago I had a close encounter with death that tested everything I had ever believed or preached about the power of God.

It all started in peace and tranquility. Perhaps my senses were lulled by the beauty of that August Friday afternoon. With my daughter, Christine, and her college roommate, Maria, I had motorboated to a small uninhabited island off the west coast of Florida. We anchored our outboard skiff behind a wooded point and went searching for shells.

The island was deserted. We strolled the sugar-sand beach looking for the swirling beauty of a Fighting Conch shell or the iridescent spiral of a King's Crown. The girls placed them in mesh sacks that had once held oranges.

After about an hour, our sacks bulging with shells, I noticed dark clouds massing in the northwest sky. At first I dismissed it as a typical summer Gulf squall that might well pass. But suddenly the sky blackened and a howling rain-studded wind struck us. Sand stung our eyes and white caps foamed angrily out beyond the beach.

"We'd better get home!" I yelled, and we raced along the curving beach to the boat. On rounding the bend, we gasped. The boat was adrift! It must have dragged anchor. Now it bobbed crazily about a hundred feet from shore.

In thoughtless panic, I dashed into the waves and began swimming frantically toward the boat. Without it we couldn't get home!

After thrashing through the high waves to where I thought the boat would be, I raised my head. It was gone. For an instant I caught a distant glimpse of its prow as it scudded before the high wind and strong current.

Then, to my horror, I realized that these same forces were sweeping me out to sea. I was powerless against them. Lifted on the wave, I spotted the girls' frightened faces on the rapidly receding beach. Their fear infected me, and I began thrashing about, fighting for my life in a foaming maelstrom.

Choking on salt water, I tried to swim, but I was helpless—the water was being churned up too much to make any progress. I berated myself for stupidity, for not making the boat secure, for trying to catch it when I should have known better.

Struggling in the seething water, I felt I would never see land again. Strength drained from me. A deep desolation filled me as my fifty-one-year-old muscles weakened and I felt myself about to sink.

Strange, random thoughts whirled through my mind. I had just paid for extensive and costly dental work. What timing! My family could have used the money to bury me.

Memories of the past flashed through my mind. I had always been proud of being able to cope with life. But now this was too much for me—I felt sure I would drown.

Then, I did two sensible things. I removed my tennis shoes. And I prayed.

"Lord, I'm going to drown. I'm coming home. I didn't think it would be this soon, but thank you for all the good things you have given me in this life. Wonderful wife, family, friends. Thank you for my ministry and outreach for Jesus Christ."

Immediately I seemed to sense God speaking. There was no voice, but the thought distinctly entered my mind: *Who says you are going to drown?*

Something strong and alive filled me at the thought of these words—a hope, an assurance that God was with me no matter what.

With this hope came renewed energy. Instead of sinking I found myself treading water. *The waves are high,* I thought, *but the water is warm and I can stay afloat like this for a long time.* Lightning ripped the black sky as the storm raged. But I was calmer. I felt stronger.

I glanced at my luminescent waterproof watch. A whole hour had gone by since I had swum for the boat. And still the storm raged.

I continued treading water. Something bumped my leg, and panic swept over me. Sharks? An unuttered prayer of helplessness shuddered through me, and the fear subsided as I held on to the Lord's presence. I was not touched again.

Hope was keeping me alive! I recall the familiar words: "And now abideth faith, hope, and love" (1 Corinthians 13:13). Strangely, I had often written and spoke on the importance of Christian faith and love, but somehow I had never personally realized the power of hope or addressed myself to it.

Now I knew there was physical strength in hope. Prayer was keeping me in direct contact with the Lord, and the sureness of his presence fed my hope, which was renewing my strength.

The roar of the sea and wind increased as another long hour went by. Two hours in the sea with waves seven to eight feet high—and I was still alive!

Then through the darkness I saw a strange apparition. It appeared to be a large Christmas tree coming toward me! Soon I recognized the illuminated mast and triangular rigging of a large seagoing tug. Hope soared. My salvation!

Exultantly, in the trough between the waves, I raised my arms, waving and shouting: "Over here! Here I am! Help! Help!"

Soon it was only a hundred feet away, its lights ablaze, engine and propellers drumming in the water. But the storm drowned out my voice. And the tug passed on by, its glowing stern lamp disappearing in the darkness.

I slumped in the water in despair, hope and strength draining from me. "This is it, Lord," I gasped. "I guess I'm not going to be saved after all."

The reply came in my mind: *Two hours ago, when there was no tugboat, you placed your hope in me.* Like lightning across the sky I felt God's test upon me: *Do you put your trust in the tugboat . . . or in me?*

"Forgive me, Father," I murmured, and again energy flooded me and I continued treading water. Another hour passed. Still another hour! It was a miracle that I was still afloat. Four hours in a storm at sea. Cramps were starting to grab my legs, but the sky began to lighten and the wind seemed less intense.

I reached for hope once again.

Gradually the storm passed and the Gulf sparkled a brilliant blue under a late-afternoon sun, and suddenly there on the horizon was the tug hurrying toward me, white foam surging at its bow.

I knew it would come. Totally exhausted now, I knew that hope alone buoyed me up.

When they lifted me on board, the old grizzled captain explained that the girls had signaled him from the island with their bright orange sacks.

"I was praying to find you," the captain said, "but to tell the truth, I was looking for a body." He peered at me closely and exclaimed: "My word! I've never seen such stamina in an old man."

I tried to smile and flopped on the deck, my back against a cabin, as I looked out at the water and thanked the One who had been with me out there. I had been careless in not anchoring the boat securely, and foolish to swim after it. My only right move had been to place all certainty of hope in God.

The next day I sought out the old captain to thank him again. I learned that he had been retired for some time and had only put out to sea to fill in for someone else the day before.

He had been pushing two oil barges when he spotted the girls' signal. Miraculously, he understood what they were trying to communicate and radioed the Coast Guard for permission to cut loose the barges and hunt for me. The Coast Guard also sent out a twenty-five-foot boat, but the storm was so severe they had to turn back for one twice as big.

The tug captain confessed to me that early the previous day he had run aground in the Inland Waterway. "Terrible on my record," he said, grimacing, "but you know what? That delay was what put our tug in the right place at the right time so we could rescue you. And for that I thank God."

So did I!

TEN

The Dam's Broken!

BY DAVE EBY
TOCCOA FALLS, GEORGIA

Our house spun like a top. How would I save my family?

The rain was coming down in torrents that night, as the wind howled and a terrific thunderstorm raged. Eventually the storm knocked out the electricity for the campus of Toccoa Falls College where I am the Dean of Men. We live on the campus, which nestles in the gentle foothills of northeast Georgia. Our house is located across a street and a creek from the men's dormitory, Forrest Hall. When the lights went out for a few hours, at around 9:30 P.M., several guys in the dorm took advantage of the darkness to play some practical jokes. The victims of these pranks were not amused and tempers flared. So for several hours I had to deal with those problems. It did not make my day any better.

November 5, 1977, had not been a good day for me at all. My wife, Barbara, had put some things on layaway for the kids' Christmas gifts with money we simply did not have, and the kids had gotten on my nerves at supper.

I went to bed around 12:30 after watching a little TV to help me relax. But it would be a night I would never forget. For up on the mountain, above the 186-foot-high Toccoa Falls, a fifty-five-acre man-made lake was relentlessly gnawing at the old dam with the pressure of 176 million gallons of water. Finally, at 1:30 in the morning, with a tremendous roar, a wall of water burst through the dam, unleashing some 700,000 tons of irresistible fury. With unbelievable speed, this juggernaut raced down the mountains and through the forest crushing trees like matchsticks.

Faster and faster it rushed to the lip of Toccoa Falls where it plunged the 186 feet at an estimated 150 miles an hour.

Barb and I were awakened by what I thought at first was an earth tremor. But Barbara jumped out of bed and yelled. "The dam's broken!"

"You're crazy," I retorted as I pulled the curtains apart to look outside. The water looked higher, and as my eyes adjusted to a streetlight I suddenly realized the water was almost level with the house windows.

As Barb ran through the playroom to get the kids, the nightlight went out as a result of a transformer upstream being engulfed. However, she managed to grab Kim, our older daughter age seven, and bring her back to me in the bedroom. Then she rushed back to get the other two children, Kevin, five, and Kelly, two.

I decided to try and break out through a window in the bedroom so Kim and I could run up the mountain beside our house. In my anxiety I did not even notice the gash I inflicted on my arm at this time. To make things worse, there was plastic on the other side of the glass and punching through that was like hitting Jell-O.

Meanwhile, Barb had gotten the other two kids, whose room was on the corner of the house nearest the creek. They were in the hallway running back to our bedroom when a thirty-foot wall of water swept over the house. A slimy brown liquid accompanied by a sickening stench began pouring through the windows.

The house groaned as it was ripped off its foundation. Floorboards buckled, walls were torn out of place, and even the carpet was peeled off its base. The tremendous force of the water twirled the house downstream like a merry-go-round. This violent circular motion prevented Barb and the kids from ever reaching our bedroom. They were forced out into the living room where they grabbed onto four spindles that connected a five-foot-high wall divider to the ceiling.

In the meantime, the water had pushed Kim and me through a bedroom door into a utility room that we had added to the house. Then the floor lifted up and shoved us against the ceiling by the back door of the room. Barb could hear us struggling as we tried to get out.

The whole utility room then broke off from the rest of the house. This kept Kim and me from being crushed and drowned. But now we were also thrown out into the water. Somehow in the darkness we were washed up against the house and I caught hold of the roof.

The house continued spinning through the waters for about fifty yards until it wedged itself between the heating pipes of what had been an old warehouse.

Eventually I was able to put Kim on the roof and then climb up myself. Although we were safe for the moment, I thought for sure that Barb and the other two kids were dead. I tried to prepare Kim for this. I told her I was afraid the others were lost. She nodded silently, as if she understood.

Sitting on the rough surface of the roof, we watched the swirling waters shatter the music building across the street. A little while later I saw the roof of the utility room floating nearby. I thought that if we could leap on it, maybe we could somehow paddle it over to safe ground. So I coaxed Kim to climb up on my back, paused for a second, and then made a frantic leap. Unfortunately the roof went to pieces when I landed on it, and Kim fell off. The water closed over my head.

Then, in the next few moments, I experienced something I will never forget. I thought to myself, *My wife is gone, my kids are gone, and I'm the only one left. Nobody knows I am under this cold, filthy water. Nobody knows my pain and sorrow.*

But suddenly, in that moment of the most awful loneliness I have ever experienced, I felt God's presence. He knew I was there and that was enough. If I died, I knew I would be with God and with my family.

At the same time, I felt two small arms grab my neck and a frightened little girl's voice say, "Don't let go of me again, Daddy!"

Somehow just hearing Kim's voice gave me new strength. We bobbed to the surface and hung on to the awning that had been part of the door to the utility room. A wild hope came to me that maybe if we were still alive the others might be too. I began shouting for Barb at the top of my lungs. To my amazement, through the roar of the water came a happy voice that sounded far away. And then two other little voices started yelling excitedly. Soon, the whole family was shouting in joy that we were all still alive.

But the danger was not over yet. The force of the water was still powerful and we were getting weaker by the minute. Barb's arms were becoming numb from the strain of having to hold the kids and herself.

We then decided to pray that God would either allow the water to drop quickly or that he would bring death painlessly. We had to yell at the top of our lungs to be heard, and even little Kevin was praying with the rest of us.

Within seconds, it seemed there was a definite shift in our house and the water seemed to drop quickly to a safer level. There was also a quiet conviction that with God's help we had made it.

By now we could see people on the other side of the water, so we started yelling to them. Eventually several ambulances and fire trucks arrived. Someone shouted, "How many are there?"

I yelled back, "All of us!" A cheer went up from the other side that almost drowned out the subsiding roar of the water.

It was then I felt a warm trickling on my arm and looked down to see it was covered in blood. A paramedic yelled out to wrap it as tightly as possible. So, grabbing a sheet that had miraculously remained in the house, Barb and I bandaged it securely.

Suddenly I saw the beam of a flashlight that was coming down the hillside behind our house. As the figure came out of the woods, I recognized Greg Bandy, a university student who lived about a hundred yards upstream. His house was on higher ground and had suffered little damage.

In a few minutes Greg was leading us through the woods, over briars and stones, back to his house. We were all barefoot and had little more than wet, dirty sheets to cover us, so the dry clothes and warm blankets awaiting us at the Bandys felt great.

When Barb and the children were dry and comfortable, Greg and I hiked downstream where the water had now dropped low enough to expose a fallen log. We crossed the stream. On the other side, I was greeted by Ken Sanders, the Dean of Students. After a joyful and emotional reunion, he said grimly, "We can't find three of the boys."

This was only the beginning of the bad news. As I sat in the emergency room of the county hospital getting nine stitches in my arm, ambulance drivers and rescue teams started to quietly carry in stretchers with bodies wrapped in white sheets. The flood waters had taken the lives of 309 people that night and injured 60 others. About half of those fatalities were children—some had played and gone to school with my kids.

Since that unforgettable night, I think I can honestly say that my life has changed. The little taste of the reality of God that I got during that moment of unbelievable loneliness has developed in me a thirst to really know God and stay close to him, not just in moments of crisis, but in the quiet moments of everyday living.

To be quite honest, I was pretty bored with life before the flood. Now I realize what a marvelous privilege it is just to be alive and to love God and serve him.

Several months after the flood, a minister was visiting the school and I was asked to give him a tour of the campus and the damage. Afterward, as he was getting out of the car, he said something that I'll never forget. He said, "Remember, the same God who was with you in those moments of peril will be with you in the doldrums of life."

I know he is—and I'm bored no longer.

ELEVEN

Jump!

BY GEORGE RIVERA
BROOKLYN, NEW YORK

No ladders. No firemen. Just one pair of waiting arms.

I was leaning under the hood of my car, starting to take out the carburetor, when a guy I knew came into the garage, laughing and joking around.

"Hey, man," he said, "you ought to go outside and check out the fire down the street. A guy jumped out a window and cracked his head on the sidewalk."

I pulled my head out from under the hood and looked at him. "I'm glad you're enjoying it," I said sarcastically and frowned.

"Hey, don't get uptight. I was just kidding—no one really jumped." He shrugged his shoulders and sauntered out.

He shouldn't talk like that, I thought. *It's not right.*

But then, not much was right, it seemed. I was a mechanic for the New York City Department of Sanitation, but I didn't go in that day—I thought I would work on my own car. My stomach was cramped and achy and I couldn't face the prospect of crawling under one of those filthy trucks, breathing in gas fumes and the stench of years of garbage hauling. A couple of times I had been sick and almost fainted. I had missed a lot of work because of my stomach, but all the doctors could recommend was that I get another job. Money problems, health problems . . . nobody cared. And not far away a building was burning down.

I shut the hood of the car and put my tools away, thinking I had better go and see what was happening.

As I walked outside, I passed little groups of people standing around on the corners, drinking and high on drugs, though it was only 10:30 on a cold December morning. I had lived here in Brooklyn for ten years and had seen the neighborhood change as people moved in and out so fast you couldn't learn their names. People remained strangers, not wanting to get involved in anybody else's problems.

My own brother had been stabbed to death in a senseless brawl on a street very much like this one. José had been my best friend. We went everywhere together. He made sure I went to church and took communion.

"The good die young," he used to say bitterly, trying to understand.

Yet with God's help I had slowly come to accept his death. Still, a feeling of deep regret stayed with me. If only someone had cared enough to stop that fight . . .

Now, as I rounded the corner, I saw the smoking tenement building and a crowd of frenzied, excited people in the street. Some were staring up at the top floor, shouting and waving their arms, and some were just standing there, crying helplessly. As I ran nearer I could see the reason for their terror. Two little girls were stuck on the fourth floor—the top floor. We could see their heads amid the choking black clouds that surged out of the window and I could hear their terrified screams—"Help! Help! Get us out!"

I felt as if they were my own kids—they just had to get out.

"Has anyone called the fire department?" I asked a bystander.

"Yeah. They should be here in five minutes."

That'll be too late, I thought, and ran into the entrance of the building. The heat was so intense I thought I would suffocate.

I ran outside again to see that a couple of teenaged boys had gotten a ladder. But it leaned pitifully inadequate against the building, not even reaching the second floor. Something had to be done fast.

Surprised at the hoarse, urgent sound of my own voice, I began screaming to the girls, "Jump! Jump! I'll catch you!"

"You're crazy, man," someone shouted at me. "They'll kill you if they land on you—that's a forty-foot drop! Wait for the fire truck!"

He must have thought that my five-foot-four, one-hundred-pound frame couldn't take the impact of catching the girls from such height.

Then someone else said, "You could kill them, too, if you drop them or miss them—don't be a fool!"

But I ignored them both. There was no time to waste. I had felt how hot it was in that building and I could see the smoke getting thicker and thicker every second. "Jump! Jump!" I yelled.

The smoke was now so thick I could hardly see the girls—I doubted that they could see me either. "God," I prayed, "help them! Give to those girls the courage to jump! Help me catch them, God! Send them straight into my arms! Give me the strength to catch them!"

Suddenly I spotted one of the girls hurtling down toward me feet first. With a tremendous thud the forty-five-pound child crashed into my outstretched arms and chest. I buckled, but held on to her with all my might as we fell onto the sidewalk. Scrambling to my feet, I gave the girl into the hands of her neighbors. She seemed to be unhurt.

"Are you all right?" I asked her. Tearfully, she nodded yes.

I looked up at the window for the other girl. By now the smoke was so thick I could see no sign of her. "God guide her fall. Don't let me miss her," I prayed again. Something told me to move backward a few feet. "Now, you—jump!" I screamed. "I caught your sister! Don't be afraid!"

Up on the ledge, the girl stood still for a moment, crying, gazing blindly into the smoke. Then she jumped.

The impact of her sixty pounds, plummeting from forty feet, sent me reeling once again back onto the sidewalk. But I held her firmly in my arms—I had caught her and she was all right.

We were helped to our feet by the crowd, everyone talking at once, asking, "Are you all right? Are you all right?" The two girls were in each other's arms, crying with relief. Flashbulbs went off in our faces. The reporters had already arrived, and a few minutes later the ambulances, fire trucks, and police came.

In the midst of all the excitement I felt sure and calm. I knew for certain, maybe for the first time in my life, that God was with me.

We were taken to the hospital and checked for injuries. The two little girls and myself were completely unhurt. I learned that their names were Pamela Polsunas, eight years old, and her sister, April, seven. They had been spending the weekend at the apartment of their mother's friend, who had left them alone for a few minutes while she went to a nearby laundry.

Except for a slight scratch on April's cheek, they had no cuts or bruises at all. It was miraculous. Sometime later I came across the verse, "The eternal God is thy refuge and underneath are the everlasting arms" (Deuteronomy 33:27). It answered my questions of how I could have caught those girls as they dropped from such a height, and where I got the strength and courage. Somehow I knew that underneath my own arms were the arms of the everlasting God, holding me, keeping Pamela and April safe.

Since that day things have changed for me. A lot of my bitterness has been taken away. Not because of all the attention I got—the story was on the radio and TV news and in all the papers—but because God showed me how much he cares for all of us. My health problems have cleared up and I have been able to work steadily. I am planning to continue my education on the G.I. Bill. What I see on the streets and the hard times in my life that I remember—these things don't haunt me anymore. I just try to do my best because I know that God will uphold me. He cares.

TWELVE

The Silent Swamp

BY MARVIN ROBERTS
CLEARWATER, FLORIDA

Everything was green—green cypress, green vines, green water—and I was lost in it.

The smell of frying bacon woke me. I turned to read the luminous dial of the alarm clock on the bedside table. It was 3:30 A.M.

Mary, my wife, entered the room. "Come on, Marvin," she whispered. "Time to get up."

Our sixteen-year-old son, Jim, stood behind her. In one hand he held the streamlined collapsible bow and four razor-pointed arrows that we had been practicing with for the past year out in the backyard. In the other he held my brand new cap-to-boots camouflage outfit that I would soon be wearing for the first time.

I knew how badly Jim wanted to be included in this, my first hunting trip. I was an experienced woodsman and fisherman, and the central Florida swamp where I was headed called for pretty much the same basic outdoor skills. The truth is, I was looking forward to mastering it. Still, I wanted to get a firsthand feel for the swamp—all

42,000 acres of it—before including Jim in any expeditions.

At 4:00 A.M. I kissed Mary good-bye and pulled out of the driveway to pick up my partner, a good friend from work. We had decided to hunt in teams of two. An hour later, we met with the others and parked our trucks on one of the elevated unpaved grades that penetrate the Green Swamp Wildlife Management Area. From these, a network of smaller grades spread out and into the misty green waters where bears, bobcats, coons, and 'gators made their home.

"Hey!"

My partner had spotted a set of wild boar tracks. They looked like a pair of big ones, too, by their size and deep impression. Farther on, the trail forked, with one set of tracks leading to the left, the other to the right. Excitedly, we split up, not an uncommon thing for hunters to do, agreeing to meet back at the trucks no later than 4:00 P.M.

For an hour or so, I followed the tracks until they disappeared. I was ankle-deep in swamp water. The hot Florida sun had burned away the morning mist and, as I slowly turned around, it was easy to see how the Green Swamp had earned its name. Everything was green. Green cypress trees towered overhead, in some places so dense they blocked the sun. Green vines, thick and tangled and full of thorns, hung from the tree branches. Velvetlike moss coated the cypress stumps and fallen logs, and the water, a murky brown, was covered by a green blanket of cypress blossoms.

The high-pitched buzz of crickets filled the air and I headed back—slightly chagrined that, with the morning only half gone, I would most likely be spending the rest of the day sitting in the truck waiting for the others to return.

My boots were soaked. Looking down, I noticed with alarm that the water, once ankle-deep, was now halfway up my calf. Ten minutes later, it was up to my knees. I felt a bump against my leg. Something underwater had hit me. The water, I knew was full of snakes—and rattlers—and for the first time I appreciated my heavy protective leggings. I tried to hurry, but an underwater grid of submerged logs and slippery rocks made the footing treacherous and my progress slow.

I was worried. Somehow, I had lost dry land and wandered deep within the swamp. The sun, now high overhead, was hot, but I felt a chill that went right to my stomach. I yelled, loud and long, for my friends. There was no answer. The dense foliage blotted up my cry like a sponge.

"Don't panic," I told myself. But my head was spinning. I had to get out of the water. I slogged over to a fallen log, pulled myself up and sat. "Collect your thoughts," I tried to calm myself. "Assess your supplies."

In the excitement of the hunt, I had left my walkie-talkie, along with my compass and matches, in the truck. I did have my bow and arrows and, strapped to my belt, the Bowie knife Mary had given me two Christmases ago. I dug into my pants pockets and pulled out a small stick of mosquito repellent and a tube of first-aid ointment. In my jacket I carried a canteen of water and a ham sandwich.

My only directional indicators were the sun and a sluggish westwardly current. Using these for a compass, I lowered myself in the water and continued west. Soon, however, I was waist-deep in the mire. I felt a knot in my stomach as I realized that those curious floating logs weren't logs at all—but alligators!

Suddenly, my left foot dropped out from under me. I tried to pull it up, but it was pinned between two underwater logs. Struggling to get it free, I saw with horrifying clarity the potential danger of my situation. Was this to be my grave?

I wasn't ready. It couldn't be true. I could take care of myself. No swamp was going to do me in. In anger, I gritted my teeth and yanked my foot from its trap, wrenching my ankle and tearing the flesh. Searing pain traveled like a skyrocket up my leg and exploded in my head.

Using my knife, I hacked my way through the tangled mass of vines. In some places, I had to turn sideways to squeeze through the cypress palisade. As I continued, the vines seemed to grow thicker. The water inched up to my chest. Looking back, there was no trace of my path, so quickly did the vegetation close in around me. And then, in terror, I realized that I wasn't making progress. I was trapped. I could go no farther. Like a fly in some hideous web, I wriggled and squirmed and pushed against my captor.

I was helpless. For the first time in my life, I couldn't take care of myself. I felt shame for the uncontrollable scream rising from the bottom of my lungs. But, more than noise, it took a form and shape that surprised me. From the depths of my soul, from some hidden place that had never before been tapped, my desperate cry rang out through the swamp.

"Lord!" I summoned, "I'm giving this to you. Take my fate and do with it what you will!"

The swamp was silent.

But a strange peace came over me. Someone had heard. I was sure of it. I wasn't a regular churchgoing man, but I knew God was in that swamp with me.

Two words seemed to dance in my head, replacing the pain from my wound. It was a sentence, I realized, from the Bible—a two-word sentence that made sense, no matter how I said it: "Pray constantly" (1 Thessalonians 5:17, RSV).

Over and over, backward and forward, I repeated the phrase. It seemed to give me renewed strength and confidence. I took firm hold of my knife and swiped at the wall of vines. They fell around me. I took a step. And then another. To my amazement, a passage opened through the tree trunks. In the dusky twilight, I went on.

I spent the night high in the treetops, lashed to the branches with my belt. In the inky blackness, I listened to the long, slippery sound of things sliding from the branches and dropping to the water, and to the eerie cries of nameless nighttime terrors.

I prayed constantly.

In the morning I waited for the sun to burn away the mist, climbed down from my roost, and continued west. My water ran out the second day. I had to drink the swamp water, murky, sulphur, and infested with parasites. I strained it through my T-shirt and jacket. I prayed that I wouldn't get a fever. Once that day, I entered an open area where thousands of yellow grasshoppers flopped about like locusts. One climbed up my walking stick and on to the back of my hand. It was food. I pinched off its head and ate it. I also ate crickets and the tender shoots of air plants, which fortunately grew in abundance among the trees.

Sometimes, search planes would fly so low I could read their registration numbers. I tried using my metal canteen as a reflector, shining it in the sunlight, hoping they would see its flash. At one point, when a rescue helicopter was buzzing the area, I used all my strength to climb to the top of a very tall tree. I cut off its upper most branches and removed my shirt to make myself visible. I sliced a strip of leather from the sheath that held my knife to my belt and fastened it to the end of an arrow. This, I knew, would cause the arrow to fly in a gyrating, attention-getting path. Finally, the 'copter came so close, I could see the pilot's face. I shot my arrow. He never saw it.

Still, I kept on praying.

On the third evening, as I began the exhausting climb to my berth, I looked over my shoulder at a wondrous sight. There, in the lavender haze of twilight, was a river that stretched as far as the eye could see.

Tomorrow, I thought, as I lashed myself to a sturdy limb, *tomorrow, I'll just catch a log and float down that river to home. Home . . . to Mary, and to Jim.* Wrapped in the security of morning's promise, I waited patiently for the long night to pass. But when dawn finally arrived and the mist burned away, there was no river. I had imagined it.

"Lord," I whispered, "you've taken me this far . . . ," but I didn't have the strength to finish. Confused and weak, I pressed on. The water, I noticed, was getting shallow. My pants, exposed to the sunlight, were beginning to dry. My footing became more sure, my progress swift. And suddenly, I was standing on dry ground. Ahead was one of the elevated grades.

I half-stumbled, half-ran to the rutted, muddy path that would take me home. I dropped to my knees and thanked the Lord for seeing me through. Not too many minutes later, I heard what sounded like gunshots. I shouted in their direction, and then I saw a Jeep coming down the road. It was a game officer and a volunteer. They had fired their guns to get my attention. They were blowing their horns and yelling. It was a mighty pretty sight.

I don't remember too much between then and waking up in the hospital. When I opened my eyes, Mary was beside me. She held my hand.

"It's not a dream," she said. "You're really here."

I started to cry. A lot of reporters were outside, wanting to talk, but Mary sent them away. She had our Bible with her, and she read to me. The words were soothing, like honey. She said they had given her strength and comfort when I was gone. It was the Ninety-first Psalm.

"Now you don't need to be afraid of the dark any more," she read. "You can safely meet a lion or step on poisonous snakes . . . for the Lord says, 'Because he loves me, I will rescue him'" (TLB).

Nearly two years have passed since Mary sat at my bedside and read to me. True to the words of the psalm she had read, I am convinced that it was because I trusted in the Lord that he rescued me. Since then, I guess you might call me a regular churchgoing man.

But, even more important, I try to make a special effort to call on the Lord always—not just on Sundays, or in times of trouble. That lesson—along with the smell of swamp water in my pants and jacket that no amount of washing can remove—will be with me forever.

THIRTEEN

The Hand on My Shoulder

BY JERRY BOND
ATLANTA, GEORGIA

The little girl was in terrible danger. I had to help her—but I couldn't do it alone.

Late one March evening in 1974 I was wakened by the sound of distant cries and shouts. At first I thought it was a domestic quarrel, but an urgency in the voices caused me to think it might be something more serious. I got up and opened the window. The smell of smoke, heavy and pungent, drifted into the room. And the voices, shrill with panic, cut clearly through the cool night air.

"Help me! Help me! My little girl is in there!"

Alarmed, I pulled on my pants, grabbed a flashlight, and followed the cries to Medlin Street, a block and a half away. There the house of a family named Green, a one-story brick structure, was ablaze. Black smoke was pouring out of the windows. A small crowd had gathered, mostly neighbors and a few policemen. The fire department hadn't arrived yet.

In the flickering orange-black gloom, I watched in horror as a team of men worked to pull Mr. Green, severely burned and in a state of shock, through a small window near the back of the house. Then I saw Mrs. Green and three of her children huddled together on the front lawn. Their faces mirrored fear and terror. Mrs. Green was hysterical.

"Theresa!" she screamed. "My Theresa is still in there!"

I've got to do something, I thought. *I've got to help.* But I stood there frozen, unable to move. Confusion and panic surrounded me, became a part of me. The whole atmosphere seemed to crackle with heat and tension. I was afraid. A great shower of fiery sparks lit the night sky as part of the house caved in, and I heard Mrs. Green scream again.

"Oh, Lord," I prayed, "please help me." Then I rushed to the house and pushed my way through the first available window. Once inside, I could hardly see. My heart was beating like a drum. Everything was black and smoking.

I groped my way forward until I got halfway across the room. Then, abruptly, I stopped. Something—some strong and strange sensation, told me that I was in the wrong room. *This isn't right,* it seemed to say. *This isn't where you'll find her.* The feeling was so powerful that I couldn't shake it. And then, I felt on my shoulder the sure, firm grasp of a hand pulling me back toward the window.

"Get out of here!" I yelled, fearing for the other person's safety. I turned to follow, but there was no one there. There was only myself, alone and trembling.

Gasping, I headed for the window, pulled myself through, and lowered myself to the ground. I looked up to see Mrs. Green's frantic eyes desperately searching my own for encouragement. Finding none, she gestured wildly toward another window.

"There," she whispered hoarsely. "Go in there."

The window was a few feet off the ground. Someone gave me a boost, and I pushed myself inside, dropping to the floor with a thud. This room, too, was dark and smoldering. My eyes were smarting. I could barely see an arm's length ahead.

"Oh, Lord," I prayed again, "please help me."

What happened next left me momentarily stunned. First, as if in answer to my prayer, I felt a surge of confidence that I was, indeed, in the right place, that I would find Theresa. And then, to my amazement, I felt the return of the same firm force on my shoulder that had pulled me from the other room. This time, however, it was even stronger and it seemed to push me to the floor. Though I didn't understand what was happening, I didn't fight it. Instinctively, I let it take over. Its presence was both calming and reassuring. I knew it was good.

I relaxed, and let myself be pushed to the floor. I began to crawl, following the wall, arms outstretched, reaching, grabbing. I came to a bed and raised myself to search its rumpled surface.

No! a voice seemed to warn. *Stay low!* I returned to my crawling position. I had found nothing on the bed. *Don't worry,* the voice whispered. *You're almost there. Don't worry.*

At the foot of the bed lay a great pile of charred chairs, quilts, and blankets that seemed to have been thrown to the floor by someone in a panic. Reaching deep into the tangled maze, I found what I had been looking for—an arm, a leg, it was impossible to tell—but I knew I had found Theresa. I pulled and pulled until she finally emerged, a limp little brown-haired bundle. She was badly burned.

"Theresa?" I whispered.

A shuddering gasp, barely audible, confirmed that she was alive. I threw her over my shoulder and ran for the window.

The crowd outside stared in silence as I gently laid Theresa on the ground and began to administer mouth-to-mouth resuscitation. Her small face, black with soot and burns, was expressionless. Blue lights from police cars pulsated in the darkness. As I breathed into her tiny frame, I prayed for her survival. Wailing sirens and flashing red lights announced the arrival of fire trucks. I kept on breathing and praying. I listened to the fire chief bellowing orders on his bullhorn, and then I heard the front door being kicked in. The fire, reignited by the fresh supply of oxygen, exploded with a scorching blast.

Theresa's eyelids fluttered. She was breathing on her own. I held her until the ambulance arrived.

"Looks like you got her out just in time," said the medic, as he took her from my arms. "She's burned pretty badly, but she'll be all right."

I waited for the ambulance to pull away, and then returned home.

Shaken by the experience, plagued by the smell of burning flesh and the echoes of terrified screams, I couldn't sleep. More than anything else, I was completely unnerved by the mysterious Presence that had led me to the little girl. I had always had faith in God and in the power of prayer, but this kind of intervention seemed uncanny, too close for comfort—at least for me. The idea was too much to comprehend, but I couldn't dismiss it. It kept me up all night.

At 7:00 A.M. I put on a jacket and shoes and returned to the scene of the fire. The house, a charred hull of blackened brick, was still smoldering. Skeletal shells of smoking furniture were strewn around the front yard. The fire inspector was there with a few policemen. He asked me what I was doing there. I told him. He said the blaze had probably been caused by a cigarette left burning on the living room sofa.

I went around to the room where I had found Theresa. Like the rest of the house, it was badly charred and blackened from smoke. The walls were blistered from the intense heat. In one corner rested the remains of a melted tennis racket.

Slowly I turned to gaze around the gutted room, when suddenly I stopped, transfixed—my eyes riveted on the wall. There, directly above the spot where I had found Theresa, was a portrait, neatly hung and, strangely, the only thing in the room undamaged by the fire. The frame, to be sure, was black with soot, but the face, the calm, steady, reassuring face, was clear and untouched.

It was a picture of Jesus.

To this day, I don't know how long I stood there, incredulously returning the portrait's gaze. But when I left, it was with newfound understanding that I whispered my thanks.

FOURTEEN

The Door

BY ROBERT L. DAUGHERTY
DANSVILLE, NEW YORK

On the other side was an inferno. How long would we be safe?

I slipped off my eyeglasses and smiled. I had been watching my wife's sister and my namesake brother-in-law decorating their apartment. It was great sharing the holiday season with Barbara and Bob Kirkpatrick. My wife Harriet and I had faced a rather lonely Christmas in the snowy isolation of upstate New York last year, until we received the invitation to spend a vacation with the Kirkpatricks in Dallas. Their apartment was in the plush and modern Athena Complex.

"There'll be plenty of room," Bob had promised.

So we came, just in time to trim the tree and help with other last-minute preparations. And the early morning hours of the day before Christmas Eve found Harriet and me sleeping soundly in the guest bedroom.

A scream from my brother-in-law woke us.

Still in our nightclothes, we opened the door to the living room. A glowing orange haze contrasted eerily with the darkness. Bob, sounding strangely distant, shouted something about a fire.

"We'll look for a fire hose!" I heard him call. Then I heard the metallic sound as he opened the steel door that led from the apartment to the outer corridor.

Attempting to follow his voice, Harriet and I bumped, then crawled aimlessly in the half-lit surroundings.

"This is dangerous," I pointed out. "It's all strange—if we go out in the hallways, we might get lost. And we don't know where the smoke is coming from. Let's sit tight in the bedroom until we know what to do."

We were still huddled in the bedroom waiting for the Kirkpatricks' return when the electricity cut out minutes later.

"Don't worry, Hon," I said, though I was also trembling. "I'll see what's happening."

I swung the door open and couldn't believe my eyes. Fire had already swept into the living room. The hot breath of flames flew at my face. It was all confusion. My first instinct was to grab Harriet's arm and attempt a run through the flames. But I hesitated. We could easily get hurt, or lost in the smoky, unfamiliar corridors.

"Lord, please help me make the right decision," I prayed.

Whatever choice I made would be fateful. Fourteen floors up, there would be no escape if we stayed in our bedroom. There was no exit from it—only one window, and no terrace. Yet something, almost against reason, forced me to go back there, to slam the door behind us.

As our eyes grew accustomed to the darkness, Harriet saw the telephone on the night table. She sprang for the receiver and held it eagerly to her ear. Only gradually did she lower it.

"No dial tone," she choked finally. "The line is dead."

Her words were interrupted by a great crash and roar from the next room. We both gazed at the wall. It was as though some living evil lay beyond it, trying to force its way in.

Fearfully, we both began to pray without hope, without plan. We just asked, "God, please be with us." Even that did us good. Our composure was better after praying. And now my mind was working.

"God hasn't forgotten us—look, Harriet!" I said, gesturing with conviction at the doorway. "That's a steel door he gave us. Flames won't eat through steel. If we barricade it shut—and keep everything else good and damp—we should be able to keep out the flames a little while. Until help comes."

Feverishly, we set to work. Somehow, Harriet helped me shove a heavy wooden dresser against the door. Then we turned on the faucets in the bathroom that adjoined the bedroom. When the tub and sink overflowed we let the water soak the floor and carpet of our thirteen-by-fifteen-foot room. Meanwhile, we tore up towels, soaked them, and stopped up the ventilators where smoke was streaming in. As another precaution, I used my shoe to smash open the fastened window. December air whistling in gave us an odd chill despite the growing heat.

At the window, Harriet and I both called for help. But our cries were lost in the night air.

"Oh, Lord, what do we do now?" I prayed.

For the first time, I noticed a plastic wastebasket, floating out from beneath the bathroom sink. "We'll use that to wet down the walls!" I exclaimed. Harriet nodded. Silently, we took turns from then on, splashing bucketfuls of water against the bedroom walls. At one point, we pulled the bedspread off and plunged it in the tub. We intended to hang it by the door for further protection. But we had to give up the idea when we found that even the two of us couldn't lift the heavy sodden spread.

Harriet went to the closet farther along the wall from the door. She felt inside. "This back wall is awfully hot!" she said. So we splashed that with water, too. At first, it was an activity of minutes. But the minutes added up, and stretched incredibly on. Soon we would have been trapped almost an hour. In our growing state of terror, we didn't talk much, to avoid the panicky sound of our own voices. Hopelessly, Harriet lay on the bed and presently covered herself with blankets preparing a rest period. *Maybe I can save her,* I thought, *if I tie enough bedsheets together and lower her through the window.* I mentioned the idea to Harriet.

She shook her head.

"We're on the *fourteenth* floor. Besides," she added, "do you think I'd ever leave you?" She rose from the bed with new determination. "We'll stay. The door will keep the fire out of here, with God's help," she said.

The walls of the room were steaming alive. Beyond them, popping and crashing noises told me that surrounding rooms—the living room, kitchen, and master bedroom—were furnaces now, incinerating their contents. "God," I prayed, "will the floor be next? Or these walls?" But, like Harriet, my thoughts returned like a magnet to the door. Unreasonably, it seemed to symbolize safety from the holocaust around us.

"Yes, we can stay safe in here, as long as we keep wetting things down and wailing for help," I said. Water splashed on the walls sizzled hotly now. If the bedroom overheated much more, I knew it could burst into flames. Helplessly, I located a jewelry box and hurled it to the pavement far below our window. But this was a back street. The crowds of evacuees from the building had assembled behind fire lines forming on a main street in front of the building.

"They don't know we're up here," Harriet moaned. "We're lost."

Heartsick, I held her in my arms. For the first time, I believed it was over too. We crouched as drifting smoke filled the upper part of the room. But we resolved to keep splashing the water. And then, a final disaster, Harriet slipped and fell on the wet bathroom floor. Bones in her ankle were either broken or badly dislocated. She could hardly move.

When I saw the sickening swelling of Harriet's leg, I no longer thought of escape. Everything now depended on God's protection. The fire sounded like some hellish whirlwind just beyond the steel door. I remember thinking that it was the only thing that kept death away. No more talking—we wrapped in wet blankets, we held each other in our arms. No more talking—we just silently prayed. An odd thought occurred to me then. After coming all the way to Texas to avoid a "lonely" Christmas—at a moment like this—we had found that all we needed for comfort was to be together.

Then suddenly, amid the deep roar of the flames, we heard an ominous new sound. Like thunder.

Harriet recognized it first. "It's water . . . water! Firemen's hoses!"

We screamed together. In a few moments our rescuers were pounding at the bedroom door. Gratefully, we shoved the heavy dresser aside and collapsed into their arms. I have only the dimmest recollection of the tortuous route that we followed, in and out of black rooms and dark hallways and, finally, outside.

It was ended. But there was an aftermath.

Next day, while Harriet rested her injuries (her ankle was treated for fractures), I accompanied a fire marshall—and my brother-in-law, Bob—back to the fourteenth floor of the Athena to survey the scene of the blaze.

"When Barb and I came back after looking for a fire hose and saw all those flames, we were sure you'd left already," Bob explained.

"Only later, when we couldn't find you on the street, did we start to really worry. A fireman told us, 'There's no way anybody could be alive up there.'"

The near-accuracy of that statement made my stomach feel queasy when I saw the apartment again. The walls were charcoal. Heat generated by the fire had been so intense that it had consumed everything in the room. Where the Christmas tree had been, where sofas and chairs and tables had stood—there was now only ash scattered on the floor. Even the porcelain fixtures were gone.

Only the room where Harriet and I had withstood the siege was nearly intact. I pointed to the blackened door.

"That steel door," I began. "It saved . . ."

My voice broke off. I shook uncontrollably as I watched the fire marshal swing the door open, flaking dark chips off the outside. The door that had looked like solid steel was hollow—and it was *made of wood!*

I thought about the conviction I had held the terrible night before. Keep splashing water around and stay behind the safety of that door. There had to be a reason that that flimsy door had not burned through. And there was only one answer for Harriet and me.

Someone whose protection was more powerful than steel had been with us that night.

FIFTEEN

My Fight for Life

BY JEAN-PIERRE HALLET
MALIBU, CALIFORNIA

The explosion had left me dazed and bleeding. I was alone in the jungle. The nearest help was miles away. Or was it?

All my life I have been in love with Africa. Helping its people—especially the vanishing Pygmies—and preserving its magnificent wildlife heritage has been my special dream.

On this particular day, as a sociologist and agronomist working for the government, I had been trying to save the Mosso tribe from famine by dynamiting fish in Lake Tanganyika. Six native fishermen and I had gone out in pirogues (canoelike boats) to do this and in the past three days had been able to fill the cooking pots of the tribe with enough silvery *ndagala* (small, herringlike fish) to stave off starvation.

This was to be our final day and I was about to throw one of the last charges, two sticks of dynamite taped together. My technique was to stand in the pirogue, light the fuse, and throw the dynamite into the lake where the underwater explosion would stun thousands of fish, which would float to the surface. The crocodiles would thrash after them but we would still get most of the harvest.

I held my lighter to the fuse and waited for the familiar crackling noise. It wouldn't light. Seconds passed. Suddenly, there was a fast hiss . . . and a vast shattering explosion that hurled me into the lake.

Almost choking, I broke surface and tried to rub my eyes with my right hand. For some reason I couldn't. I ducked my head into the water, which washed away the blood flooding my left eye. My right one was blind. And then I raised my right arm and stared, unbelieving. My hand and wrist were gone.

Burning pain filled my face, neck, chest, arms, and hand. I raised my left arm out of the water. The hand was still there, but the thumb and first two fingers were split open.

Blood was pouring from my severed arm. My terrified helpers had disappeared, evidently thinking I had been blown to pieces in the blast. Now grim ripples were arrowing toward me, the ominous waves of crocodiles.

I struck out toward shore in an awkward crawl, keeping my flexed right arm pressed tightly against my ribs, rejecting the pain that seared through me with every move. Near shore, the first crocodile caught up with me. Having swum in crocodile waters before, I knew what to do. Assuming an almost vertical position in the water, I dog-paddled, my perpendicular target a difficult one for the giant reptiles to seize because they cannot turn their heads to the side.

Clump! I could hear the hollow clack, like the beat of a giant drum, as the great jaws snapped in the space where I had been only seconds before.

My feet touched bottom. I staggered out of the water. My knees buckled, and I fell to the sand. I lay there gasping, a wreck of a human being. My shirt was gone, my shorts in tatters. Using my bleeding hand and my teeth, I fashioned a tourniquet for my right arm from my socks and an old piece of fishnet rope I found on the ground. It slowed the bleeding, but did not fully control it.

I checked the rest of me. My face was lacerated, my scalp was slashed. Waterfowl flapped overhead, strangely silent. Then I realized I was almost deaf. I couldn't hear my own voice unless I shouted.

I had to find help fast. But where? I knew I must get to the Hôpital Rodhain in Usumbura (now Bujumbura, the capital city of Burundi) at the northern tip of Lake Tanganyika. I knew that in my condition it would be virtually impossible to make the long drive alone.

"Oh, God, help me," I prayed. "Give me the strength and courage somehow!"

Could I even get to my truck? Because of the thick jungle bordering the lake, my pickup was parked almost a mile away. I didn't even know if I could stand up.

Painfully, I struggled to my feet. The ground swayed dizzily around me. I became nauseated from pain and weakness.

I stumbled forward one halting step toward the jungle. It seemed like a gigantic victory. I took another step. Pushing aside vines and leaves, I took ten steps . . . then a hundred . . . five hundred . . . a thousand. . . .

The sun was low over the trees when I saw a small patch of blue ahead. It was the fender of my pickup. As I slid behind the familiar steering wheel, a strange terrible face stared back at me from the rearview mirror. It was encrusted with blood. As I looked into my own eyes, I realized how great the odds were against my survival. The first problem was staying conscious. If I passed out, I was sure to bleed to death before anyone would find me. But that was only one obstacle.

First, I had to back the truck three miles out to the main road. Then, I faced a two-hundred-mile drive to the hospital in Usumbura. There was a shorter way, but I had heard that the government was doing repair work on several bridges, and if any was unfinished, I would be trapped. I had to take the longer route.

But on that route was the Majejuru Barrier. It was there because an eighteen-mile section of road was so narrow and precipitous that it had to be one-way. Cars heading west in the evening must reach it by 9:00 P.M. Otherwise, traffic would be closed in that direction until 8:30 the next morning. If it closed before I arrived, I would surely die on this side of the barrier.

Squinting at the sun, I guessed it was about 4:00 P.M. That gave me five hours to drive nearly 120 torturous miles. In my physical condition, and with the condition of the road, it was a tough order.

I was very close now to the absolute limit of my endurance, and I felt myself slipping away. . . .

"Lord," I prayed, "I really need your help. I cannot make it without you. My life is in your hands." I knew that I could no longer rely on my own resources.

I turned the ignition key and the motor roared to life. Thank God I had filled the tank. I had to back the truck three miles up a jungle trail, snaking around tree trunks to make the main road. Finally I was back on the dusty road, under the open sky.

Thirty-six miles away was a mission station. Holding the steering wheel with my two good fingers, I made it to their door. A white-robed priest stepped out, looked at me and fell to the ground in a faint. I couldn't blame him, the way I looked. A little native boy cowering on the porch said all the other priests were away. I climbed back into the pickup and drove on.

Darkness was approaching, and I still had some eighty miles to travel to the Majejuru Barrier. I pushed down the accelerator and my little truck roared on. Several times I felt myself falling into a stupor. I fought back by singing and praying out loud. I began to be tormented by thirst. My whole body cried out for water.

What time is it? I had no way of knowing, but felt sure it was close to nine o'clock, when the barrier would come down. I floored the accelerator and the truck shot forward at sixty miles an hour.

Now I recognized by my surroundings that it was only about ten miles to Majejuru. But the pain searing my body was blotted out by a frightful vision. In my imagination I could see the native guard lowering the massive gate across the road, then mounting his motorcycle to start his inspection tour of the eighteen-mile strip ahead. He disappeared around a curve, leaving the huge unbreakable barrier locked immovably in place. If my vision were true, I would bleed to death waiting for the gate to open tomorrow morning.

I roared on the remaining miles in an agony of doubt. Then, as I swung around the last curve, I saw the gate. It was still open. "Thank you, God!" I cried, as I drove past, I pushed on, somehow covering the miles.

Now, Usumbura lay only thirty miles away, but thirty miles of hairpin curves that spiraled down toward the lake, thirty miles of crushed-rock road on which it is easy to slide over the side into jagged ravines 3,000 feet below.

"Help me, God!" I groaned. "Don't let me faint. Keep me going, please!" And again I seemed to hear a quiet voice speaking to me, telling me that it was not my own strength that would get me to Usumbura, but his.

With this encouragement, like an electrical current, new life surged through me. My eye and head cleared, and with renewed vigor I pressed on the gas pedal. The road was downhill now. My truck descended 4,000 feet and, rounding a curve, I caught my first glimpse of Usumbura, a shower of golden lights next to the moonlit waves of Lake Tanganyika.

I rattled across the metal bridge over the Muha River at the edge of the city. I made a right turn onto the Avenue de la Limite, drove a half mile, turned to the left, and stopped the truck in front of the Hôpital Rodhain.

I sat in the cab for a moment staring at the blood-encrusted wheel, dashboard, and windshield. Then, I struggled to get out and started for the hospital entrance. A white-clad attendant ran from the door and took my left elbow, trying to help. I shook my head.

"Thank you," I said. "I can make it."

I had already met my Helper on the road to Usumbura.

SIXTEEN

The Lonely Trail

BY DON BELL
BYRON, WYOMING

"God," I said, "I know you don't owe me nothin'. But I'm awful scared and hungry now . . ."

My horse steadied herself on the slope. I looked up at the sky—and didn't like what I saw. Snow was falling hard, and there was already eighteen inches on the ground. Winter always sets in early in the Rockies, especially in the Absorkee Range southwest of Cody, Wyoming. We had had snow here since September.

It was mid-November now. Up till a few days ago, I had been one of the guides assigned to a party of hunters going after game meat in the high mountains. At the close of the season, I had brought them back to the low corral. After I had helped the hunters unload their supplies from the pack animals, though, I had found we were short three horses from the forty head we had left with.

A horse can't live through a winter in that country of jagged 12,000-foot peaks. Everything is covered in deep snow, and a horse can't paw down through snow to feed. He might try and work down to lower country till he got rimmed in by snow, but every horse I had ever known got confused then. He wouldn't backtrack but just stand and look toward home till he starved. Or froze, maybe.

I made up my mind to go after the horses. I knew every peak and canyon of the Absorkees, so I just might have a chance of finding them. I saddled my best horse and loaded another stocky packhorse with my good bedroll, a small tepee tent, and panniers filled with enough feed, bacon, bread, and coffee to last a few days. Then I started out with my old dog Shorty tagging along.

For two days I didn't see any horse tracks but our own. The trip was rough, and the higher I got in the mountains, the deeper the snow became. Sometimes my horse wallowed belly-deep in snowdrifts on the trail. And now, the sky looked bad. I didn't like the ugly way the clouds had piled up. If I turned off the trail here, I figured I could reach the old hunting campsite, about half a mile away.

I reached the camp just at dark. By then, a full storm was blowing in. People who don't live here just can't imagine how bad a Wyoming blizzard can be. I couldn't see but a few feet in front of me, so I couldn't travel much more for fear of riding my horse right over a cliff. I figured the temperature was about zero. The wind sent the cold at my face like arrows.

"Use your head, now," I warned myself. "Life's cheap in a blizzard."

With the wind howling like it was, I couldn't set up the tepee tent I had packed. The only shelter I could find was a spruce thicket set in a little hollow, so I made for that.

I had about twenty pounds of oats still, so I divided it for the two horses. I took the panniers of grub off the packhorse and loosened the pack-saddle cinch. Then I loosened the cinch on my own mount. Next I laid my bedroll out in the hollow, and crawled inside it. Shorty came in, too, and curled up, a warm and comfortable companion at my feet.

It would be nice to have God as a companion right now, too, I thought. *I'd like to talk to someone.* But I had been a cowboy all my life, spending most Sundays out on the range. I wasn't a churchgoer, though I believed in God. I had just never learned to pray to him. Didn't seem fair somehow to bother him with my talk, since I had never done nothing to pay attention to him before. So I just talked to Shorty.

"Wish I'd eaten more on the trail today," I said. But now I couldn't find firewood, or make a fire in that wind, anyhow. So I just lay still, to wait out the storm.

All night the snow fell.

When I woke up next morning, the wind was still howling. Poking my head out of the snow-covered bedroll, I saw what I was afraid I would see—nothing. Everything was light gray. And I knew the weather wasn't about to change. I had to pass another day here, at least.

Little dry pangs were letting me know where my stomach was. But I also knew, with the snowstorm like it was, I couldn't leave the bedroll. It would be nearly impossible to find my packets of grub under the drifts, and I could get lost a few feet from the bedroll—it happens in blizzards not even this bad. I wouldn't last long exposed to that weather.

So I spent a long day in a bedroll that grew stiff with cold and was mighty glad when the whiteness all around me darkened some. By evening I was no longer thinking of the lost horses I had come up on the mountain to find. The animals I had with me were cause enough to worry. The horses had long since finished the grain I had left them, and now they gave occasional whinnies to let me know how hungry and cold they were.

My own thoughts wandered to food, too, as night fell. I thought of the hard, chewy bread I had put in the grub sacks, and the meat and the coffee.

"You don't know how thick and fine coffee tastes, do ya, dog?" I said to Shorty. He shifted a bit against my legs and licked my hand.

I couldn't get to sleep that night, tossing and turning while the wind whistled and roared. Finally, when I figured it was morning, my legs were pinned by the weight of the snow on them. But I worked my arms free and dug an opening for my head.

It was eerie. Everything was still lost in the white. I heard my neighing horses through holes in the wind, but I couldn't see them at all. I couldn't see anything.

My stomach felt tight. Hungry wasn't the word for it anymore.

Also, my feet were getting cold. I was plenty scared. It looked like this bed was going to be my burial ground too.

The blizzard never let up that whole day. As darkness approached, I knew that the end wasn't very far off. I wasn't going to get through this alive, not without help.

I stared thinking about all those churches I had never been to. I thought hard.

"God," I said at last, "I never did learn to pray. Up to now, we've never been real close, I reckon. I know you don't owe me nothin', Lord . . . but, I'll tell you. I'm awful scared and hungry now. I came up here after some packhorses that strayed off. I don't care about that no more. But, if I'm gonna pull through this alive, God, well . . . I figure it's up to you. That's all I want to say."

I didn't know if I got all the prayer said right. But I was glad I had tried. I felt calmer somehow. I still didn't know if I would make it through the night. But I no longer felt so alone.

I only caught uneven patches of sleep that night, tired as I was. In between dozes, I thought how lost I must seem to the world, all huddled in a bedroll, shivering under the snow on a mountainside in a blizzard. And I thought I was dying.

I could only judge what time morning would come. I had tucked my head deep into the bedroll, and by this time I could hardly shift about under its weight. The sounds of the blizzard had been cut off a while ago. The walls of my stomach were all squeezed together, it felt like, and I knew I'd have to chance going out for food this day. *If only the storm would show some promise of blowing itself out. . . .*

Finally, I felt it was morning. I wriggled my arms and pawed against the snow that was collapsing on my head. In a moment my head was free of the sleeping bag and I opened my eyes. I was blinking in the early morning sunlight!

The temperature was way below zero, but how much I couldn't know. I knew there was still a chance of being hit by another blizzard, so I didn't waste time making a breakfast fire. I left the rest of the supplies and my frozen bedroll lying where they were.

My fingers were stiff as wood as I tightened the cinch on my saddle horse, then mounted and spurred her to begin the long journey back. Shorty followed in our tracks. Slow as we were moving, he had a tough time lunging through the drifts after us.

When I reached the point where I figured I should turn off the main trail, several fresh sets of hoofprints had luckily already broken the trail in the direction I was headed. I wondered who could be up here making tracks, and didn't know until we caught up with the animals after a few miles. There were three of them—my own missing packhorses! All were worn out and starved-looking. They were glad to be herded down toward the winter range.

It was a mighty nice sight when I topped a ridge that evening and saw firelight glowing in the windows of a cabin at the home corral. Weak and hungry though I was, I stopped and smiled.

"Well, Lord, I thought you were only in church, but you taught me something," I said. "I wouldn't have blamed you if you just ignored me. But I sure am grateful to learn you really care about a cowboy's prayer."

And we rode down to the corral.

SEVENTEEN

The Dream That Wouldn't Go Away

BY GEORGE HUNT
PARKER, ARIZONA

Two fliers were missing. No one could find them. And then . . .

Back when I was a young livestock rancher north of Roosevelt, Utah, the news, one cold November morning, reported that a California doctor and his wife were missing on a flight from Custer, South Dakota, to Salt Lake City. As a student pilot, I had just completed my first cross-country flight with an instructor, though I had only twenty solo hours.

Paying close attention to all radio reports on the search, I was very disturbed two days later by a newscast saying that Dr. Robert Dykes and his wife Margery, both in their late twenties and parents of two young children, were not likely to be found until spring—and maybe not even then. They had been missing four days, and the temperature had been below zero every night. There seemed little chance for their survival without food and proper clothing.

That night before I retired I said a simple prayer for these two people I didn't know. "Dear God, if they're still alive, send someone to them so they will be able to get back to their family."

After a while I drifted off to sleep. In a dream I saw a red plane on a snow-swept ridge and two people waving for help. I awoke with a start. *Was it the Dykeses? What color is their plane?* I didn't remember any of the news reports ever mentioning it.

I couldn't get back to sleep for some time. I kept reasoning that because I had been thinking of the couple before falling asleep, it was natural for me to dream of them. When I finally did go to sleep, the dream came again! A red plane on a ridge—but now farther away. I could still see two people waving, and could now see some snow-covered mountain peaks in the background.

I got out of bed and spread out the only air chart I owned. It covered a remote area in Utah—the High Uintas region, along the Wyoming-Utah border. The Dykeses' flight plan presumably had to pass over this range. I was familiar with the rugged terrain, for I had fished and hunted it as a boy. My eyes scanned the names on the chart—Burro Peak, Painters Basin, Kings Peak, Gilbert Peak.

Again I went to bed. And again, incredibly, the dream returned! Now the plane was barely in sight. I could see a valley below. Then it came to me in a flash—Painters Basin and Gilbert Peak! I rose in a cold sweat. It was daylight.

Turning on the news, I found there had been no sign of the plane and the search had been called off. All that day, doing chores around the ranch, I could think of nothing but the Dykeses and my dream. I felt God had shown me where those people were and that they were alive. But who would believe me and what could I do about it? I knew I wasn't really qualified to search for them myself. I knew, too, that even trying to explain my dream to my flight instructor, a stern taskmaster named Joe Mower, would have me laughed out of the hangar.

I decided to go to our small rural airport anyway. When I arrived, a teenaged boy who was watching the place told me Joe had gone to town for the mail.

The Presence that had been nudging me all morning seemed to say, "Go!" I had the boy help me push an Aeronca plane out. When he asked me where I was going, I said, "To look for the Dykeses." I gave the plane the throttle and was on my way.

Trimming out, I began a steady climb and headed for Uinta Canyon. I knew what I was doing was unwise, even dangerous, but the danger seemed a small thing compared to what I felt in my heart.

As I turned east near Painters Basin, I was beginning to lose faith in my dream; there was no sign of the missing plane. The high winds, downdrafts, and rough air were giving me trouble in the small sixty-five-horsepower plane. Terribly disappointed as well as frightened, I was about to turn back when suddenly there it was! A red plane on Gilbert Peak, just as I had seen in my dream.

Coming closer, I could see two people waving. I was so happy I began to cry. "Thank you, God," I said over and over.

Opening the plane's window, I waved at the Dykeses and wig-wagged my wings to let them know I saw them. Then I said a prayer to God to help me get back to the airport safely.

Thirty minutes later I was on the ground. When I taxied up and cut the motor, I gulped, for Joe Mower was there to greet me.

"You're grounded," he hollered. "You had no permission to take that plane up."

"Joe," I said quickly, "I know I did wrong, but listen. I found the Dykeses and they need help."

"You're crazy," Joe said, and he continued to yell at me. My finding that plane in an hour and a half when hundreds of planes had searched in vain for nearly a week was more than Joe could believe.

Finally I turned away from Joe, went straight for a telephone, and did what I should have done in the first place. I called the CAP (Civil Air Patrol) in Salt Lake City. When they answered, I asked if there had been any word on the Dykeses' plane. They said there was no chance of their being alive now and that the search was ended.

"Well, I've found them," I said. "And they're both alive."

Behind me, Joe stopped chewing me out, his eyes wide, and his mouth open.

"I'll round up food and supplies," I continued to the CAP, "and the people here will get it to them as soon as possible." The CAP gave me the go-ahead.

Everyone at the airport went into action. Within one hour we were on our way. A local expert pilot, Hal Crumbo, would fly in the supplies. I would lead the way in another plane. I wasn't grounded for long.

Back in the air, we headed for the high peaks. Hal's plane was bigger and faster than the Aeronca I was in. He was flying out ahead and above me. When I got to Painters Basin, at 11,000 feet, I met the severe downdrafts again. I could see Hal circling above me and knew he was in sight of the downed plane and ready to drop supplies. Since I couldn't go any higher, I turned around.

Back at the airport I joined a three-man ground rescue party, which would attempt to reach the couple by horseback.

Another rescue party had already left from the Wyoming side of the mountains. For the next twenty-four hours our party hiked through fierce winds and six-foot snowdrifts. At 12,000 feet, on a ridge near Gilbert Peak, we stopped. In the distance, someone was yelling. Urging our frozen feet forward, we pressed on, tremendously excited. Suddenly, about a hundred yards in front of us, the fuselage of a small red plane sat rammed into a snowbank. Nearby, two people flapped their arms wildly.

Charging ahead, we shouted with joy. At about the same time we reached the Dykeses, the other rescue party was coming over the opposite ridge.

After much hugging and thanking, I learned what a miracle the Dykeses' survival was. They had had nothing to eat but a candy bar, and their clothing was scant—Mrs. Dykes had a fur coat, but her husband had only a topcoat. The altitude made starting a fire impossible, and at night they huddled together in their downed plane, too afraid to go asleep.

"We had all but given up, had even written notes as to who should look after the children," Mrs. Dykes said. Then, turning to me, she said, "But when we saw your plane, it was the most wonderful thing . . . our prayers answered, a dream come true."

"Yes," I said, smiling, suddenly feeling as Solomon in the Bible must have felt after he received a visit from the Lord one night in a dream (1 Kings 3:5-14).

My dream, like Solomon's, had occurred for a reason. In his own special way, God gave me that dream in order to help give life to two others. Even in the most mysterious of ways, he had shown me he is always there, always listening. He had heard my prayers and the Dykeses' prayers and had answered all of us in his own infallible way.

EIGHTEEN

Last Flight From Savoonga

BY GILBERT PELOWOOK
SAVOONGA, ALASKA

To save himself and others he would need the strength of Samson—and that's what he prayed for.

We almost didn't get on the plane at Savoonga that day last summer. Every one of the twenty-eight seats was filled, but when the airline agent explained why Abner Gologergen and I had to get to Gambell, one couple agreed to give up their seats and stay behind.

Abner is the magistrate at Savoonga, and I'm a state trooper. Together we were due in court to process a case in Gambell, a little seaside village at the northwestern end of St. Lawrence Island, 160 miles off the Alaska coast from Nome and 41 miles across the Bering Sea from Siberia. Savoonga is toward the mid-northern end of the island, and once a week a Wien Air Alaska airliner makes the three-stop round trip from Nome to Savoonga to Gambell and back.

Taking a seat next to a young boy, I settled back with a magazine. In a few minutes we were airborne. The stewardess, a young black woman, moved up and down the aisle, attending to requests of the passengers. All of them, like myself, were Eskimos from the island.

To outsiders, St. Lawrence can seem a remote and forbidding land, rocky, windswept and stark, pocked with lakes and ringed by gravel beaches that descend into the icy sea. To the Eskimo, it is home, familiar. We know the brown-stony earth and the blue waters that stretch endlessly from its shores. We know Sevuokuk, the long, flat-topped mountain rising more than six hundred feet into the air, its craggy bulk a landmark.

For centuries, too, Sevuokuk has been the home of the village's dead. Villagers from Gambell carry the remains of their loved ones up the steep slopes, place them among the rocks, and leave them to time and nature. Over the centuries, to a people living close to nature, Sevuokuk became a symbol of the mysteries of life.

Many Eskimos are Christians now, and during the nearly forty years of my life I went to church and believed in God. But he had never been very real to me, and from time to time I had the vague feeling that I was missing out on something important in life.

This missing element was one of the reasons I had changed jobs three years earlier and joined the state patrol. All my life I had wanted to help people, but along the way I had gotten sidetracked. Maybe working as a law officer I would have more opportunity to give of myself, I thought.

As we neared Gambell, I glanced out the window and noticed I could no longer see ground because of fog. Then, as if from nowhere, houses appeared right beneath us. We were very low. Much too low! Suddenly I knew with a heart-clutching urge of fear that our line of flight was toward Sevuokuk, hidden in the fog.

I grabbed my seat belt and jerked it tight, then covered my head with my arms. I felt the nose of the plane rise as the pilot frantically tried for more altitude. But it was too late. There was a terrible crash. Then everything went black.

When I came to, I was upside down, held to the seat by the belt. Everything was quiet. No sounds of life—no crying or moaning. I tried to determine if I had any bones broken. I seemed to be all right.

Others were not so fortunate. When the plane hit, the seats had torn loose from the cabin floor. Other passengers, still belted to their seats, were piled upside down, beneath me, behind me, on top of me. The boy who had been sitting next to me was now fifteen feet away.

Now I could hear a noise—the sound of flames crackling. We were burning. I reached for my seat belt fastener but couldn't find it. I couldn't get to it, there was so much twisted metal.

I pulled at the belt. Nothing happened. I strained and turned. I still couldn't reach the buckle.

The crackle was getting louder and I could feel the heat. Growing more desperate, I strained all my weight against the belt. Nothing worked.

When I knew there was no way out, I began to pray. "Lord, take me quickly!" While I was praying I asked for forgiveness, for things I had done and things I had failed to do, for the times I could have helped somebody and hadn't. As I prayed, a peace seemed to come over me.

Then a small voice spoke from the calm. I could hear it plainly. Was it real? I looked around.

The voice was Estelle Oozevaseuk's. I could see her. Her lips were moving. She was praying in our Eskimo dialect for God's mercy. *There are others alive!* I thought.

Now, instead of asking God to take me quickly, I prayed, like Samson, for strength. "Help me, God. Help me reach Estelle." I got a tight grip on a piece of metal that I thought might free me and pulled so hard that I could hear the joints of my arm crack. Strength seemed to flow into me and I kept pulling with all my might. All at once the belt flew loose. I pushed with my legs to get clear of the wreckage. I twisted and crawled free.

I moved to Estelle. Her legs seemed to be broken. I released her seat belt and began easing her out of the plane, through the torn metal. Out on the foggy mountaintop, I set her down a safe distance away from the burning plane.

Through the fog I could see that the airliner had slammed into the slope just below the mountain's crest, hitting with its nose up. Then it had ricocheted up through the rocks, turned up on its nose and fallen over backwards in a heap, with the tail broken off. Flames were bursting from the wings and cabin.

I knew the people in Gambell must have seen the plane and heard it crash. They would be coming to help. But it would take them at least half an hour to scale the mountain's forty-five-degree slope.

The fire was making little explosions and growing bigger. The whole plane could blow up any minute.

Estelle and I were the only ones out. If there were any other survivors, I knew they had to get out now. I couldn't wait for the villagers. Something in me was afraid, but there was also something stronger than fear, a feeling I had never before experienced that gave me courage.

"Lead me to those who can be helped," I prayed.

Back inside the wreckage, I shouted to the people in the cabin, "Is anybody alive? Where are you?" Whenever I saw someone move, I would free him from his seat belt and lead or drag him to the opening in the plane. I kept shouting, trying to rouse the unconscious ones. "Hey! Hey!" One passenger was held in by a tangle of metal. I pried it apart with my hands and pulled at his jacket with my teeth to move him from his seat.

A new explosion rocked the plane, and I ran frantically from the wreckage. Then I thought it must have only been an oxygen tank blowing up, and I went back in again.

The fire was very hot now, and the flames were getting closer to the people. I ripped a large piece of aluminum from the plane's wreckage and held it like a shield in front of me to keep the flames and heat away. Then I found Abner, who was badly injured, and, placing the shield between him and the flames, I grabbed him and tugged. My hand stuck to his thick jacket as the melting nylon turned to sizzling jelly in my grasp. I freed him from his seat and flopped him onto my shield, then dragged him out among the rocks.

How many more can there be? I wondered. The fire was growing bigger and bigger. I could smell the fuel. It must have drenched the ground. My hands were hurting now, but I took my shield and went in again.

In the broken tail section I found the stewardess, screaming for help and hanging upside down, tangled in the metal of wire and cables. Close by, the left engine was burning, the magnesium fire giving off a greenish-blue light. I pulled at the metal, but I couldn't move it enough. I stopped, rested, and tried again. She twisted, then was able to slide free. I was afraid her back might be broken, so I tried to be careful when I moved her.

I knew I could not go on much longer. I was exhausted. My hand was burned and full of pain, and I had injured my leg on a jagged piece of metal. I sank to the ground. I had no idea how much time had passed since the crash, but I knew help would have to come soon if the other survivors were to get out. *The villagers,* I thought, *where are they?*

At that very moment the first villager came scrambling over the crest. It was Leonard Apangalek. He and two other boys had run all the way from the village, then up the steep mountainside.

Now other village people were coming, too. I hollered to them. I was so glad to see them. Though they were completely out of breath, having run the whole way from the village, they went right to work. Many of them were National Guardsmen, trained in first aid, and they knew what to do with the injured. They moved into the burning plane and pulled out the remaining passengers, dead and alive.

By now the whole area was on fire, and the villagers moved the injured back from the flames. They put together makeshift splints and stretchers from the wreckage to help get the people down the mountain. I was the last to go. By then the plane was completely consumed by fire.

We were all taken to the schoolhouse in Gambell, given additional first-aid treatment, then flown to the hospital in Anchorage by a Coast Guard plane, which fortunately was near enough to reach Gambell shortly after the crash.

Of the thirty-two persons aboard the flight from Savoonga, twenty-two of us had survived. Diane Berger, the stewardess, was the only member of the crew to live. She and Abner Gologergen and several others would have to spend weeks in the hospital, but the doctors said they would recover.

Recently my job took me back to Gambell, and I paused for a long look at craggy Sevuokuk Mountain. No wonder generations of natives have thought of it as "the mountain of the dead." But now, for me, I realized it symbolizes life, for it was on that mountain that God became a reality to me, a personal, caring God who gave me a strength and courage beyond myself—supplying the power to minister to others when they needed my help.

NINETEEN

"We Are Going to Die, Aren't We?"

BY MELVIN BITTER
FRANKLIN, MASSACHUSETTS

For seven hours they clung to the capsized boat.

The park rangers warned us that the lake was treacherous and that its winds changed suddenly. So when Gertrude and I pushed our nine-foot sailing dinghy across the sandy beach on that calm August morning, we fully intended to stay within a few hundred yards of the shore.

We were camping in Maine's Sebago Lake State Park, eighty-eight square miles of beckoning water. As stronger air currents caught us and began to bear us along more swiftly, the sensation was so exhilarating that we forgot our caution and went with the wind, out toward the center of the lake.

Then we noticed that swells were coming up from behind and overtaking us. We must have covered about three miles when I decided we had better turn around into the wind and head back. As the dinghy swung, the rudder pin snapped and the line holding up the sail broke.

I managed makeshift repairs and we began to tack toward the shelter of the shore. The lake was now being whipped by a stiff breeze. A sudden gust caught the boat broadside and we capsized. Gertrude and I found ourselves gasping in the chilly water.

Even then we had no feeling of panic, for we were both good swimmers. Each of us had a lifesaving seat cushion and we even managed to right the boat, but the waves, now about three feet high, just ran over it. There was no way of bailing it out and we decided there was a better chance of being spotted with the white bottom of the boat uppermost—which also made it easier to hold onto.

We hung there in the heaving water and waited. After fifteen minutes we were shaking from cold and knew we had to do something to generate heat. We started pulling the boat toward the nearest shore, about two-and-a-half miles away, struggling against the wind and the waves.

Occasionally other boats passed near us, but the waves hid us from them and the wind carried away our shouts. Several times we waved our cushions at small planes that flew over us, but they didn't notice us. After two hours of battling, we realized that the shore was as far away as ever. Wind pressure against the boat was canceling out every stroke we made. We decided to abandon the dinghy and swim with the seat cushions.

We realized that we were doing a dangerous thing—water-safety experts strongly recommend staying with a capsized boat—but we had tried that and it hadn't worked. Now we prayed that God would make someone concerned for us. We repeated together the Twenty-third Psalm. As we said, "Yea, though I walk through the valley of the shadow of death. . . ."

Gertrude suddenly felt panic clutch at her heart. "We are going to die, aren't we?" she asked.

"We've prayed for help," I answered. "Now we've got to believe that it's coming." But I, too, feared that we weren't going to make it.

Soon we could no longer see the boat. As we clutched our cushions and kicked and stroked with our free arms, we thought we were beginning to make progress. Then cramp pains, light at first, but quickly growing in intensity, began to cripple my legs and stomach. I had recently been in the hospital for treatment of ulcers.

We agreed that one of us had to try to reach the shore. Gertrude was in much better shape than I was, so with great reluctance she left me and swam on ahead. I watched her pink blouse crest one wave after another until I could see it no longer.

Now I felt a loneliness I had never experienced before. My whole body was wracked with spasms from the cold water. Suddenly I heard what sounded like a cry of desperation from Gertrude. "Help! Help! Help me, Help me!"

I screamed into the wind, "Trust! Trust! Hold on!" My words were whipped away. I cried desperately to God to take care of her and somehow found the strength to begin swimming again toward the spot where I had last seen her. But I couldn't see her pink blouse, and now I was sure she had gone under. I thought of the agony of telling our six children and her parents that Gertrude was dead. The temptation came to let go of my cushion and sink.

But into my mind came the words, "Call upon me in the day of trouble: I will deliver thee, and thou shalt glorify me" (Psalm 50:15). So I began to call upon God, out there in the loneliness and the wind-filled emptiness of the lake. I cried to God in my pain and suddenly my body flooded with waves of warmth. I realized that I was being warmed and encouraged by a power not my own. God came into my loneliness and filled it with himself. No human help came, but the horror was taken away.

Then dimly through the fog of my mind I heard some voices. I had wanted to hear voices for so long that I was sure it was a delusion. Then a woman's voice said, "He doesn't see the rope—I'm going to help him." Suddenly she was beside me in the water, putting a rope under my arms. And strong hands were reaching out of a boat and pulling me over the gunwale.

"Is there anyone else?" one of the men asked me.

"My wife . . . if my wife is still alive, she's out there," I said and drifted into semiconsciousness.

Vaguely I heard the men talking of switching to the other gas tank. The woman who had jumped into the water now lay on top of me to try to warm my shivering body. The boat engine was silent while the gas tanks were switched, and then we were moving. It seemed only moments before the men said, "There she is!" and one of them called, "We've got your husband—he's alive!" Then Gertrude's head was next to mine.

"Thank God, oh, thank God," I kept hearing her say.

Back at the shore, warm sand was heaped around me and blankets were put on both of us. Gertrude asked the time. It was ten after five. "Seven hours," I heard myself say. "Seven hours in that water."

I heard Gertrude ask someone, "How did you know we were out there?"

"Your boat washed ashore on a beach where we were having a picnic," a man answered. "We weren't sure there'd been an accident, but we felt we'd better check. That's how we found your husband."

"And how did you find me?" Gertrude asked.

"We had to cut off the engine while we switched gas tanks," he answered. "The wind pushed us right to you. It's really amazing."

But I knew it was more than that. It was the answer to prayer.

TWENTY

Little Boy Lost

BY DONALD G. SHAFFER
SOMERSET, PENNSYLVANIA

The raging torrent roared on to a whirlpool forty feet deep—yet I knew I had to plunge in.

The blaring ring of the telephone jarred me awake. I looked at the clock—3:15 A.M. On the other end of the phone. I heard the voice of Bill Barnhart, Somerset's fire chief.

"Don," he said, "there's a report of a drowning down at Swallow Falls State Park, in Maryland . . . a little boy. They need some people down there to help. Can you get your scuba boys together?"

Oh, brother, I thought. *Just what I need at three o'clock in the morning.* But as a volunteer scuba diver for the fire department, I knew the commitment I had made.

"I'll see what I can do," I answered. Surprising, especially since it was the Sunday of Memorial Day weekend, I was able to round up eight other divers, and an hour later, still rubbing sleep from our eyes, we met at the firehouse.

We were briefed on the facts. The boy, ten, had been wading with his father early Saturday evening in the treacherous Youghiogheny River, just above Swallow Falls, in the Backbone Mountain area of western Maryland. Suddenly the boy had been scooped up by the raging current and swept over the falls into a whirlpool forty feet deep. His father dived into the raging pool below the falls in an attempt to reach the waterfall, but was unsuccessful and barely escaped the torrents of water himself. Then he organized a search party along the shore, but again to no avail.

I shook my head sadly at the thought of the little fellow's fate. It sounded hopeless. Then I heard the chief say something that made me realize why we were all there in the middle of the night.

"Since no body has been found, there's a chance the boy may still be alive somewhere," Bill said. "Until we find him we can't be sure he's gone."

Riding in our rescue truck on the hour-and-a-half trip over the border to that isolated area in Maryland, I thought about how there had been several drownings near Swallow Falls in recent years. While I had never visited the falls, I had heard tales of their ferocity, especially at this time of year, the high-water season.

Then I thought about the boy. Was it possible he was still alive? In the darkness of the truck, I shivered. I teach Sunday school and try to believe what I teach. Yet, at the same time, prayer comes awfully hard for me. It has always been a struggle for me to ask God for something. Yet traveling down the back roads of Pennsylvania that morning, I felt a great need to pray. Closing my eyes, I murmured, "God, if that boy is still alive, all I ask is that we be given the chance to rescue him."

We reached Swallow Falls just as the sun was coming up. One look at the place confirmed my worst fears. About ten feet high and a hundred feet across, the falls tumbled down with a deafening roar into a lake-sized stream—the rain-swollen river. Near the middle of the stream was an ugly whirlpool, sucking and swishing around like a giant funnel—an awesome sight.

It seemed foolhardy to enter water like that. Standing on a rock, I watched in silence until my back-up diver, Rick Ross, appeared alongside me.

"Don, I'm really scared," Rick said. He didn't have that much experience as a diver. None of us really did. I had taken up scuba diving only seven years before after a vacation in the Bahamas. Once I got involved in the sport, I was hooked. I had taken lessons at the YMCA and then joined the scuba rescue team the summer before.

But I had never had to save anybody and I certainly had never ventured into water like that.

"Rick," I said, "I'm scared, too. But we can't let our fear beat us."

Our first plan was to have me swim under the falls. With my diving gear on, I attacked the pounding water four times. Each time I was beaten down and thrown back into the stream.

Next, we strung a rope, shoreline to shoreline, across the top of the falls. Attaching another rope to that line in a T fashion, I stayed in the water and tried to guide my way through the falls. This too proved fruitless. The charging water bounced me around like a piece of sponge.

We were discouraged now, and running out of ideas.

Working quickly, we next tied a rope to a rock upstream, above the falls. Hanging on to the rope and still in my scuba gear, I pulled myself through the falls to the rock face in back. I felt my feet land on a thin ledge of rock. Just then the rope locked in the rock face above me, so I had to let go of the rope, leaving myself with no means of getting out. Completely out of sight now, I had no trouble imagining what the other men must have thought when they saw that lonely rope float by without me.

Inching my way along the ledge in back of the falls in water up to my chest, I found myself in an eerie corridor, walled in by an ear-shattering cascade. All my shouts, I knew, would be in vain.

Suddenly I looked up and gasped. *The boy!* There, on a small ledge about one foot above the water level, was the boy. At the startling sight of him, I gave a noiseless cheer and felt goose bumps crisscross my arms and legs.

Wearing only a bathing suit, the boy was lying on his side on a stone notch carved out by the force of the water. Apparently, after going over the falls, he had been swept up in there by the whirlpool. It was an incredible landing spot, only big enough for one small person to recline on. *Surely,* I thought, *God's hand must have placed him there.*

My heart was pounding as I neared the boy. His eyes were closed. *If he opens them,* I thought, *he's going to see me and panic.* Here I was in this spooky place, all decked out like a creature from outer space. It would be enough to scare anybody, let alone a little boy who hadn't seen another soul for twelve hours.

Trying to keep cool, I approached the boy. Quickly he rose up, frightened. I worked my way over on the ledge and put my arm around him.

"Are you all right!" I asked.

"Yes," he said, his blue eyes glowing brightly. He was cold, but seemed calm.

"OK," I said, knowing that we seemed to be trapped. "We're going to ask God to get us out."

The boy needed no coaxing. Turning over, he put his palms together and bowed his head. I did the same.

"Dear God," I said, "please help us to get out of this alive."

I knew it was one thing to ask God for help, but it was another to actually survive. My first thought was that perhaps we could "buddy breathe" our way out—that is, pass my air regulator back and forth. I had to reject that idea, though. It just didn't seem like we would have the time or be able to coordinate the action. Our only answer was for me to use the regulator and hold the boy at the same time. He might swallow some water, but I hoped not too much.

Holding the boy in my right arm, I eased myself along the ledge the way I came in. I was hoping to find a place in the falls where the water pressure was weakest. As we went, occasionally being blasted by a sheet of water, I had to admire the boy for acting so calmly.

A few moments later, the ledge I was standing on dropped and my air tank caught on the upper part of the rock behind me. We couldn't go forward or backward. I knew what that meant. We would have to go straight through the full force of Swallow Falls.

I looked at the boy. He was quiet. I pointed to the roaring tumult. "We're going to have to swim through that," I said. "Take a deep breath."

"OK," he said. Again I was amazed by his courage. He swung his body around to face me, locked his hands around my neck, his legs around my waist. With all my power I pushed off with my legs into the thundering water and in direct line of the whirlpool.

As we struck the main thrust of the falls, we were driven down, down, down into a swirling, bubbling blackness. After about fifteen seconds of being pitched about, I began kicking my flippers desperately. It was a race against time. I had to get the boy's head above surface.

Fighting my way up, I took the boy by the waist and with every ounce of my strength I thrust him upward in a catapult motion. I was suddenly glad for all those years I had worked in the concrete business. Hauling heavy blocks and stone by hand had given me power in my arms, but even so, I was amazed at all that instant strength.

As the boy shot up past me, my regulator was knocked loose and water began pouring down my throat. It didn't matter, for suddenly, I too, was rising to the surface.

When my head broke the water I heard wild yelling and screaming. I looked around and saw a diver jump from a rock and grab the boy. We had made it! We had missed the whirlpool by inches!

In a few seconds a rowboat was by my side. Still gagging water, I grabbed onto it. I felt a strange mixture of weariness and joy.

Later, when the boy's father reached me by telephone to express his gratitude, I learned that the family lived outside Washington, D.C., and had been visiting Swallow Falls when the near-tragedy occurred.

The boy's name, I learned, was Richard Bouchard. It wasn't too long before I got a chance to visit Richard. He's a swell little guy who loves baseball, and, believe it or not, swimming.

Though neither of us really mentioned the rescue when we talked, I know neither of us will ever forget it. It is an experience both of us will always cherish, something that comes along once in a lifetime. God, in bringing two strangers together in an improbable and dangerous place, heard our plea and gave each of us the courage to find the way out. Richard and I will always be bound by that struggle, but even more, we will be tied by a knot of faith that can't be broken.

TWENTY-ONE

Kidnap!

EUNICE PETERSON KRONHOLM
LINO LAKES, MINNESOTA

Startled, I turned to face two men wearing masks.

The air had a brilliant clarity that cold Friday morning in March as I stepped out of the house. I was still not feeling well after a week's siege with the flu, and I shivered despite my heavy wool pantsuit, coat, and scarf.

My husband, Gunnar, had left for work and I was now leaving for an 8:15 A.M. hairdresser's appointment. We live in a suburb of St. Paul, Minnesota, and our house is somewhat secluded. I was scraping ice off the car windshield when I heard noises. Startled, I turned to face two men in ski masks. One pointed a nickel-plated revolver at me. I screamed. They lunged at me and wrestled me into my car.

"Do what we tell you and you won't get hurt," one commanded. I was paralyzed with fright. They blindfolded me, tied my hands, and shoved me down in the backseat.

"What do you want?" I gasped as the car surged out of the driveway.

"We'll tell you later!"

The horror of my situation swept over me. There was no one at home. Our children are grown and live elsewhere. Gunnar didn't expect to hear from me until two o'clock. I found myself praying, "Father, I trust you to watch over me."

After about an hour of twisting and turning, then being transferred to another car for more driving, we entered a garage. I was led upstairs into a room. Peeking under my blindfold, I could see a white shag rug.

"Sit down here," a voice ordered.

"Please, what do you want?"

"Money—from your husband."

Of course. Gunnar was president of the Drovers State Bank in South St. Paul.

"Where can we reach him?"

After I told him, he said grimly, "If everyone cooperates, it shouldn't take but a few hours."

One of the men left and my other captor sat down beside me. I could sense his tension. Thoughts of recent kidnapings in which desperate men killed their captives chilled me. I tried to blot them out, and as I did, Bible verses came into my mind. Two verses from Isaiah kept coming to me: "Fear thou not; for I am with thee. Be not dismayed; for I am thy God. I will strengthen thee" (Isaiah 41:10), and "Thou wilt keep him in perfect peace, whose mind is stayed on thee: because he trusteth in thee" (Isaiah 26:3).

As my fear subsided, my senses seemed to sharpen. As a nurse who teaches classes in mental health, I decided the best thing was to talk to him, to try to keep things calm.

Trembling inwardly, I tried to sound lighthearted. "Well, I don't want to talk to the wall. So I'll call you Bill. OK?"

Silence, then a muttered, "OK."

"How much will you ask for?"

"Half a million."

Half a million dollars? My heart sank. "I don't know how my husband can get that."

"He'd better!" The voice was ugly.

I prayed inwardly for Gunnar, then started rubbing my wrists where they had been tied.

My captor shifted toward me. My nostrils picked up his rough scent. "You're a cool one. How come you're so calm?"

"Because I believe God is protecting me."

He was silent. But strangely it seemed a receptive silence. So I told him how Christ had changed my life and given me a new set of values. He didn't respond, but I thought I sensed a change.

It was now probably about noon. He gave me some coffee. I was still blindfolded, but I could hear a radio monitoring police calls. In the afternoon the other man sat next to me. "I called your partner Bill," I said. "What can I call you?"

"Jerry will do."

Hour after hour we sat. My body was aching. By now they must have reached Gunnar. Surely they would let me go soon.

I forced myself to talk to Jerry. I asked about his family. Then he turned to me with almost the same question that Bill had asked, "How come you're so relaxed?"

"God gives me strength to endure," I answered, trying to keep my voice from trembling. "I believe in his protection. Do you want me to tell you about it?"

He jumped to his feet and walked away. "No," he snapped.

The slow minutes ticked away. Evening had come. Bill returned.

"Have you reached my husband?" I asked. He mumbled something about being double-crossed. "You'll have to spend the night here," he said.

Here? Tears welled up. But again came reassurance: "God is our refuge and strength, a very present help in trouble" (Psalm 46:1).

Now hunger pained me. I had had no food since breakfast. Jerry gave me a tiny bit of a sandwich, saying it was all he had.

I spent a fitful night on the rug. By Saturday morning every bone in my body ached. Both men seemed grim. Apparently the ransom arrangements weren't going as expected.

Still nothing to eat or drink. At noon one man handed me a can of soda.

Late Saturday, Bill said, "We'll have to move you." They took me to the garage. The icy air bit into me. I heard the car trunk open.

"Please!" I cried. "Not the trunk!"

"It's the only way," Bill retorted. They thrust me in, then slammed the lid. I lay hunched around the spare tire as we bumped over rough roads. Hours passed. I cried in pain from cramps and the cold. Finally we stopped, and, still blindfolded, I was led into a small room.

I was handed a stale wiener bun. I ate one half and saved the other. Two days had passed. Would I ever see Gunnar again? But again that comfort: "He that keepeth Israel shall neither slumber nor sleep" (Psalm 121:4).

Sunday morning Jerry guarded me while Bill left. I was coughing from the flu. Jerry snapped on the radio.

"Can you get KTIS?" I pleaded.

KTIS is a religious station, and soon a familiar hymn from the First Baptist Church came over it. My heart lifted. I knew the minister, Bill Malam, and his wife, Rita. Then came a special announcement. "We ask all listeners to pray for the safe return of Eunice Kronholm." Suddenly I felt much better.

My Sunday dinner was a can of soda. Later that day, letting me lift my blindfold for the time it took, Bill and Jerry made me write Gunnar instructions on delivering the ransom.

That night they tied me up, then both left to pick up the ransom. I lay there sick with fear. My fears came flooding back. Then abruptly Bill returned and said, "We've got to move." We got into the car again.

Maybe I'm going home! I thought. But after driving awhile, we parked and I was led into a strangely familiar room. Under my mask I could see the white shag rug. It was starting all over again!

Jerry then came in and Bill left. "When am I going to go home?" I pleaded.

"I don't know." Jerry seemed sullen. From my black world I couldn't see him, but I sensed something ominous.

Then a thought came to me. I had prayed for protection and been given it. But maybe I should ask God for a specific time of release—not just sometime, but a definite hour. The hour of 6:00 P.M. came into my mind. "Oh, God," I prayed, "Take me home by six o'clock tonight."

I relaxed. "Jerry," I said, "I don't know what you think, but I feel that God is going to get me home by six o'clock tonight."

He didn't reply. The radio music was interrupted by a special news report: "A suspect in the Kronholm case has just been arrested."

Jerry became very agitated. Fear again clutched me as he paced the floor muttering. *Is this when it will happen?* I thought. *A quick explosion behind my head? My body buried in the woods?*

I trembled, then decided to refuse to think about ugliness or death, but rather, as the Bible says, "Think about things that are pure and lovely, and dwell on the fine, good things in others" (Philippians 4:8).

Now I tried to convince Jerry to let me go. "I'll get some money for you," I pleaded.

"No," he said, "it won't work." He kept pacing the floor. It was now after five, according to the radio.

"Why don't you let me go now?"

"Well," he said, looking out the window, "wait until dark."

Until dark? I was too weak to walk in the dark. I talked to him a little longer, then said, "I think I'll put my coat on."

"OK," he said, sighing wearily, "you might as well take off your mask, too." It seemed as if something was beginning to crumble within him.

As I stood to leave, my smarting eyes blinking in the harsh light, I could see that he looked pathetic and mournful.

"You know," he said, "I've never met a woman like you. You don't seem to feel bitterness or anything."

I looked into his tormented eyes. "I have no bitterness toward you, really." I touched his shoulder. "I forgive you. God loves you."

I turned and stepped out into the dusk. As I started down the wooded road I heard him following me. A cold wind tore at my coat as I plodded on. I reached a highway, looked back, but couldn't see Jerry.

"Oh, Father, a car, please." Soon one approached and I stepped out into the road, waving my arms. The driver took me to a nearby grocery store. My fingers shook as I dialed home. One of our sons answered. Our three children were at the house waiting and praying.

The FBI men came quickly and took me to Gunnar. We fell into each other's arms. A few minutes later I looked at my watch. It was 6:10 P.M.

TWENTY-TWO

Snowbound

BY STEVEN HULT
SAN JOSE, CALIFORNIA

The five of us huddled in the backseat. The car became our icy prison.

Dark clouds threatened and the snow on the ground was being swirled around by the wind, but in Minnesota in March, what else is new?

The five of us weren't worried too much about the trip as we prepared to drive home to warm, sunny California that Easter vacation. Terrell Day, Julie Carlson, Fredda Baker, Carolyn Miller, and I, all students at Bethel College in St. Paul, piled into my car and started the twenty-six-hour journey to San Jose.

A blizzard was forecast, but the auto club told us conditions were good if we left immediately. Somewhere in Iowa rain suddenly pelted the car and didn't let up.

"It's a good thing this isn't snow," I said as I turned over the driving chores to Terrell. Exhausted from the strain of driving through the rain, I fell right to sleep.

When I awoke around 3:00 A.M., I couldn't believe my eyes. Somewhere in the middle of Nebraska the rain had turned to snow and the wind was whipping the white stuff around so hard that the road was barely visible. Terrell, still driving, was creeping along at five miles an hour.

"I can only see the sides of the road when the wind lets up for a second," he said, running his hand through his hair.

Suddenly the car ground to a stop in a snowbank. We had run clear off Interstate 80 without even seeing the edge.

"Oh, great," exclaimed Carolyn. Then, "What do we do now?" she asked, trying hard to sound matter-of-fact about it.

"Help has got to come," Julie said calmly. "We've got plenty of food, and surely a snowplow or police car will be along soon," Just then, in fact, a diesel truck passed us, then three cars. After that, nothing. . . .

It was 4:00 A.M. when we got stuck. We decided to wait for morning and get some sleep in the meantime. We had three-quarters of a tank of gas, but didn't want to waste it, so we bundled up in coats and a sleeping bag, turned off the engine, and dozed till dawn.

When we awoke the next morning, we couldn't see past the windows. A one-half-inch layer of ice coated the car and another one-quarter inch of ice covered the insides of the windows from the condensation of our breath. The storm was raging as hard as ever and every once in a while our car would rock from a gust of wind, really giving us a fright.

Time dragged. Every five minutes someone would ask, "What time is it?"

Because Bethel has a religious orientation, it was only natural for Fredda to say, "Let's all try and quote as many Bible verses as we can."

So we did. But about eleven o'clock that morning we all started really feeling the cold. Knowing better than to start a car in a snowbank, I decided to clear the exhaust pipe of the snow.

I shoved with all my weight to force the right door open against the wind. When I got out and let go of the handle, the wind knocked me to my knees. I was only a few feet from the car, but I couldn't even see it! Desperately I waited for the wind to die down before I dared to move. Finally, during a momentary lull, I made sure the tailpipe was clear and struggled back into the car.

"Welcome, abominable snowman," cracked Julie. My blond hair and beard were matted with ice, as were my coat and pants. I started the engine.

While the defroster strained to clear the windshield, we listened to the radio weather report: "Temperature is now minus fifty degrees with the wind-chill factor . . . wind out of the north-northwest at seventy miles an hour . . . storm shows no sign of letting up . . . snowplows and police cars cannot get out."

For the first time we realized we were in serious trouble.

"We've got to try and make it to the next town," I said. The map showed Chappell, Nebraska, as the closest place, but, since we were unsure of our location, we didn't know how far away it was.

After rocking the car several minutes, I managed to drive out of the ditch. But up on the road it wasn't much better. Five minutes and a hundred yards later, we were in another ditch—on the other side of the road.

This time, nothing we tried—rocking, spinning, pushing—could free us. We were trapped—and the cold was really getting to us in a wicked way. The wind forced snow through the weather stripping around the windows and through the rubber cover on the floor-mounted stick shift. We had accidentally closed a door on a seat belt that had fallen out the door, so it had frozen slightly ajar. Snow drifted through the crack and soon covered the floor of the front seat. Our car had turned into a refrigerator.

Four P.M. We had been stuck twelve hours. Since I'd been outside trying to free the car more than the others, I was feeling the effects of the cold a bit more. I felt sleepy and numb all over. I wanted to stay awake but couldn't, and I kept falling into a delirious sleep, dreaming someone was banging on the roof of the car. I would wake up hungry and disoriented, but I couldn't manage the energy to ask for even a lemon drop to eat. Suddenly, from out of my sleep, I heard the others praying.

It took me about five minutes to force myself to tell Julie. "I can't feel anything, and I can't even move."

"Quick," she said to Carolyn, "help me pull him into the backseat." With body heat, brisk rubbing, and a peanut-butter sandwich, I was soon feeling better, but we were all beginning to realize we might not make it through this ordeal.

Huddled together in the backseat, the five of us began our second shivery night. Four of us sat up and the fifth lay across our laps. Without anyone in the front seat, the steering wheel and dashboard instruments soon were coated with ice.

Except for chattering teeth, we were silent through most of the night. Once through, Terrell and Julie both said, "Maybe we should write letters to our folks. . . ." The idea cast a gloom over the already darkened car.

Frankly I was surprised at my reaction to the situation. I wasn't afraid to die. I had learned to trust God and knew he was in control. The problem for me that night was that I kept wondering, *What had my life been worth?* I kept on coming up with the same answer, *Not much, up to now.*

In the front seat I saw my tape deck and all my eight-track stereo tapes, a collection worth more than $100. The tapes had been important to me, but as I sat there freezing I thought how strange it was they had become so unimportant so fast.

Then I looked at my friends in the car with me—Terrell, Julie, and Carolyn, freshmen at school for the first time, and Fredda, the short, dark-haired girl who wanted to be a teacher. What meaningful things had I ever done for them? What had I ever done to make a difference in their lives? Very little, I knew, for I had always been so wrapped up in myself and my possessions.

While those thoughts kept running through my mind the wind shrieked outside. I hardly slept at all and I know no one else got much sleep either.

When dawn finally came, its light revealed a beautiful, peaceful scene when we opened the back window to see what it looked like outside. The car had been like a cave for us, it was so covered with ice and snow. The snow and wind had stopped, and the sun glistened on a still, white world.

Our hopes soared again. We put a yellow knapsack on the radio antenna. Julie thought we should get out a suitcase and write "Help" on it with lipstick and set it in the road. But the trunk of the car was frozen shut.

Terrell and I decided to go outside and hammer on the trunk to open it, and as I opened the car door, I saw a car coming down the highway, the first car we had seen in more than thirty hours. Frantically I waved my arms over my head. The driver slowed and stopped. I was so happy I could hardly talk. "Praise the Lord," I said.

Terrell added a heartfelt "Right on" as he scrambled out of the car behind me.

The rescuers turned out to be two young men from St. Paul on their way to Utah to ski. All five of us jubilantly squeezed into their car. They told us they had passed many stranded cars, but all of them had been empty. A short way down the road we passed an accident involving the diesel and the three cars that had passed us the first night. The ten people involved had spent the two nights huddled together in the cab of the truck.

We saw how really fortunate we were when we arrived at the emergency center set up at the Chappell fire station. We were in the only vehicle that had no one hurt or wasn't ruined. Twenty people were still unaccounted for. The people of Chappell were fantastic. They took us into their homes, fed us, and helped us go back and dig out our cars.

I never did make it home to California for Easter. Another storm moved in, stopping me from making a second attempt. But no vacation could ever replace what I learned from being snowbound.

Sitting in that freezing car, I saw how my life had to change. Before that ordeal I based most of what I did on the material possessions I could get through my actions. But being so close to death, I realized that life is a gift from God, too short to be squandered on meaningless things. There are just too many people in this world who are desperate for someone to show them God's love in a really personal way.

When my time does come, I want my life to have counted for something—more for the acts I have done for others than for myself. I want to have a lot more to offer God than I had that stormy night in Nebraska.

TWENTY-THREE

Arrest Jesse Watson!

BY SGT. NORMAN BUCKNER
INDIANAPOLIS, INDIANA

The story of a police officer and the man he wouldn't shoot.

The warrant for the arrest of Jesse Watson was similar to many others I had handled. The big difference was that two years earlier I had arrested this same fugitive. I couldn't remember much about him except that he was a big guy, tough and surly. Latest report said he had been taking drugs. He was wanted for grand larceny in both Indiana and Florida.

Then one evening last April I received a call saying Jesse Watson might be hiding out in his father's apartment in western Indianapolis. My partner Don Harvey and I went to check it out.

When we arrived at the apartment building, Don and I were joined by Sgt. Ron Bealey. Don and Ron went to the front door, and I went around to the back. Above the noise of a heavy rain I could hear someone answer their knock in front. A scuffle followed, and Ron called to me. I ran around and found that Watson had tried to close the door on them, then had retreated inside the apartment. Since I had the only flashlight and was in uniform I went in after him.

I couldn't locate any light switches and even with my flashlight I could see very little. Revolver drawn, I searched each room. The rain thumped away outside. The apartment was like a cavern inside, making me shiver.

Reaching the back bedroom, I stopped by the door. My light caught someone standing on the far side of the bed—a figure holding a blanket in front of him. It was Jesse Watson.

He was as big as I remembered, but the shadows made him seem even more awesome. At six feet two inches tall and 220 pounds, he towered over my five-foot ten-inch, 160-pound frame. A full beard gave him a menacing look.

I guessed he might have a club under the blanket. I moved toward him and said, "OK, Jesse, drop it."

"No, you drop it," he told me. The blanket fell to the floor, revealing a gleaming twelve-gauge sawed-off shotgun that was pointed straight at me. One squeeze of the trigger and I would be blasted in two.

My heart began to roll like a kettle drum. I could feel a throbbing in my temples. I managed to keep my flashlight and revolver on him but I wondered what to do. *I'm really defenseless,* I thought as I looked down the barrel of that shotgun. A picture of my wife, Joyce, and our two small children flashed across my mind. I had never been so petrified in my life.

For a moment I thought of firing—but something stopped me. Never in my twelve years on the force had I shot anybody. Suddenly, instead of opening fire, I found myself praying: "Please help me do the right thing, God."

Behind me, outside the bedroom door, I could sense Don and Ron waiting for me to make a move. I realized the reason they were holding up. Watson, they surmised, wasn't rational and might begin shooting if he saw trouble. It was better to let one person handle him. The thought unhinged me. If I was this nervous, I wondered how tense Jesse Watson must be.

For several minutes we stood facing each other. I was afraid to say anything for fear it might upset him. My throat was bone dry. "Give me strength, Lord," I prayed. "I've never been in anything like this and I'm trusting in you."

What must have been minutes later, my breathing still coming in spurts, I finally spoke again, quietly, "Jesse, your only chance is to come with us."

"No way," he answered, waving his shotgun at me.

We were at an impasse, neither of us willing to back down. More minutes ticked by. My arm ached from holding the flashlight. Then my eyes, now becoming accustomed to the darkness, caught sight of something on the bed. There lay, of all things, a Bible.

I was filled with a feeling of hope. I stared at the book. "If your Word is real, I need you now," I prayed.

"What about that, Jesse?" I said, pointing to the Bible.

"I'm going to church now," he muttered. Then with sudden authority, "And I feel all my sins are forgiven."

"That could be, Jesse," I said, choosing my words carefully. "But first you have to settle things here."

"How can a man on earth be judged?" Jesse demanded. "God is the only judge!"

I put my revolver in its holster, slowly, so Jesse could see me.

"Jesse," I said, "do you think hurting someone would be right in the eyes of God?"

I bent over to pick up the Bible, still watching Jesse. He didn't move. Flipping the pages, I had little idea what I was looking for. I could hear myself breathing deeply. I stopped at Romans 8:18.

"Jesse, listen to this!" I read rapidly: "'For I reckon that the sufferings of this present time are not worthy to be compared with the glory which shall be revealed in us.'"

Jesse was silent. He had caught the meaning for himself.

"I can't take jail," he shouted.

"Don't try to limit God, Jesse," I said. "You could be effective in jail. Look at Paul when he was in prison. And Daniel in the lions' den. You could help others get to know the Lord."

He nodded, but kept the shotgun pointed at me.

I was running out of ideas again. I glanced at my watch. Incredibly, more than an hour had passed since the stalemate had begun. My body cried out in fatigue. I kept praying silently.

Suddenly the silence ended with a tremendous explosion. The windows shook and a yellow flash lit up the room. The blast threw me back against the door frame.

Then I saw what had happened. In the long strain of the situation, Jesse's finger must have twitched and touched off the trigger. Fortunately at that moment his weapon had been pointed downward. The discharge tore a huge hole in the bed.

For a long minute Jesse didn't move. I held my breath. Then, abruptly, he dropped the shotgun on the floor.

I went over and touched him on the arm. He looked at me, his eyes moist. Then he held out his wrists so I could put on the handcuffs.

"The Lord sent a man of faith to rescue me," he said wearily. I was so exhausted, I couldn't reply.

I saw Jesse again two days later.

"I've been reading the Bible," he told me, "and I know that with God's help I'll make it." Then he apologized to me for letting the shotgun go off.

He was a different man—and so was I. Nerve-wracking as that experience was, it seems to have opened many doors for me. When other officers ask me about it, I find myself able to share my feelings about God with them. I could never have done that before.

More than ever now, I try to look on each new case as a special one. Each person—like Jesse Watson—becomes a special person. If I can reach out and help just one single human being, I know I will have done something to make my life worth living.

TWENTY-FOUR

God, Send Someone!

BY DICK SULLIVAN
STONEHAM, MASSACHUSETTS

Guideposts was ten years old when this dramatic story appeared on its cover—a strange experience that continues to chill.

At 4:00 P.M., June 14, my brother Jack was just crawling down into a ten-foot-deep-trench that ran down the center of Washington Street, a main thoroughfare in West Roxbury, Massachusetts.

It was near quitting time. Jack is a welder, and he wanted to finish one particular part of his job before he left. He said good-bye to the other men as they quit, took his welding lead in his right hand, and lowered himself and his electric power cable into the trench. His head was well below the surface of the street.

Traffic above him was heavy. Though Jack could not see the cars and trucks, he could feel their vibrations. Occasionally a pebble would break loose from the side of the trench and fall into it. Jack paid no attention to them.

It was Jack's job to weld the joints of a new water main both inside and out. First he crawled into the thirty-six-inch diameter pipe, lowered his mask to protect his eyes against the bright welding arc, then went to work. After completing the inside of the joint, he crawled out of the pipe. It was 4:30 P.M. He began to weld the outside. Halfway through the job he stood up to get the kinks out of his legs. Jack stretched, turned toward the pipe, and pulled down the shield again.

Suddenly the bank caved in. Tons of dirt came crushing down on him from above and behind.

Jack was rammed against the pipe with the force of a sledge hammer. He went down, buried in a kneeling position, his shield slammed against the pipe, his nose flattened against the inside of the shield.

He felt his shoulder burning against the red-hot section of pipe he had been welding. He tried to move it back from the pipe. But he couldn't, then his nose began to hurt. It was bleeding. And he couldn't move his head.

Jack tried calling. Three times he shouted. The sound of his voice died in his shield. He tried to breathe slowly to preserve the supply of oxygen.

It crossed Jack's mind that he might die.

Slowly he began to pray. Going to Mass at St. Patrick's once a week suddenly seemed quite inadequate. My brother continued to pray. He had his eyes open, but everything was black.

Something cool crossed his right hand. He wiggled his fingers and found they moved freely. His right hand had not been buried. He moved the hand again. He tried to scratch around with his hand to open up an air passage down his arm but the weight of the earth was too great. It didn't do any good.

Then it occurred to him that he had been holding the welding lead in that hand. So he fished around with his fingers. He found the rod, still in the holder. He grasped it tightly and moved it, hoping it would strike the pipe. Suddenly his wrist jerked and he knew he had struck an arc—the electric current would be making its bright orange flash. So he kept on tapping the pipe, making an arc, hoping it would draw attention.

That must look like something! Jack thought. *A hand reaching out of the ground striking an arc against the pipe. That must really look like something!*

He began to figure out how long he had been buried since there was no way of telling time. He wondered how much gasoline was left in the engine-driven welder on top of the trench—whether it would last until dark when the orange arc might draw attention. Then he remembered that it was almost the longest day in the year. Darkness wouldn't fall until nearly nine o'clock. Still, if he had enough oxygen in his little tomb and if the gasoline held out, maybe. . . .

He thought of all the hundreds of people passing within a few feet of him up above. He thought of his family and wondered if he would ever see his little grandson again. He thought of Tommy Whittaker, his assistant, out on another job on Route 128.

He figured there wasn't anything to do but lie there and wait and keep tapping flashes, and hope that enough air would filter into the mask to keep him alive. There wasn't anything to do but lie there and pray, "God, send someone."

In another part of Boston, out on Route 128, Jack's assistant, Tommy Whittaker, had quit his work for the day. Whittaker was forty-seven years old, Jack, forty-one. They had known each other for more than fifteen years and were close friends, so close that within the next few moments one of the strangest prayer phenomena in modern times took place.

Tommy Whittaker did not know that Jack was on the Washington Street job. Whittaker got in his truck and started off down Route 128 with the full intention of driving directly home. Route 128 is a main artery, a superhighway that could take him home within minutes.

But as Whittaker drove, he began to have the feeling something wasn't right.

He tried to shake the feeling off. He kept driving. The strange and unexplainable sensation grew. He thought that he ought to drive up to the Washington Street job and check it, then dismissed the idea. It meant driving six miles out of his way at the peak of the rush hour. Whittaker approached the intersection of Washington and Route 128.

Suddenly he turned.

He did not try to explain it to himself. He just turned.

Meanwhile Jack continued to pray. It was the same simple prayer, "God, send someone." The bleeding in his nose hadn't stopped. The blood ran down his throat and began to clot. "God, send someone." He spat the blood out, but it was getting more difficult. All the while he listened to the muffled sound of his welding motor outside. He wondered if it was dark yet. It seemed an eternity. Things were getting hazy.

Tommy Whittaker drove along Washington Street. The job was divided into two sections. He stopped his truck at a spot several blocks away from the cave-in and got out. He chatted with an engineer for the Metropolitan District Commission for fifteen minutes. Whittaker did not mention the gnawing sensation that still would not leave him alone. The time was 5:45. It was still broad daylight.

Back in the trench, Jack struck some more arcs. He thought it might be dark now. He listened to the welder popping. He hoped someone would come—soon. The clot of blood in his throat was getting harder to bring up. He was a little surprised that he wasn't in a state of panic. Jack just kept praying, "God send . . ."

Up above, a little way down Washington Street, Tommy Whittaker got into his truck, said good-bye to his friend, and started up again. The gnawing sensation grew stronger. He reached a stoplight. It was his turnoff to get back to Route 128 by a shortcut. If he stayed on Washington Street, he would have to go still farther out of his way. Tommy Whittaker braked his truck for a brief instant, then continued on up Washington.

Underground, Jack finally gave up striking the arc. It was making him breathe too hard. He didn't think he could last much longer. He couldn't get the blood clot out of his throat. He was gagging. . . .

At that moment, up above on Washington Street, Tommy Whittaker arrived at the spot where his friend was lying. Nothing seemed unusual. He noticed the stake-body truck. But it was a truck that Sullivan never used. Whittaker thought another man from the shop was down in the trench. Whittaker pulled up, got out of his truck, and noticed the welder was running. He thought someone was inside the pipe, welding. Still nothing struck him as unusual.

Then Tommy Whittaker saw the hand—and saw it move!

"Oh, God!" he whispered.

Whittaker jumped down into the trench and dug like a chipmunk with his hands. The earth was too packed. He scrambled out of the trench, looked back at the hand, and shuddered. He shut off the welder and raced through the traffic across the street to a garage.

Underground, Jack heard the pop-pop of the welder stop. It was then that he began to prepare to die. He knew it was over. He was gagging and trying to throw off the mist that had come over him.

Tommy Whittaker, just feet away, shouted to the men in the garage. "There's a man buried alive over there! Get a shovel."

Back across the street Whittaker raced, carrying a snow shovel. He ran to the place where the hand stuck up, still not knowing it was his friend.

Jack, below, felt an extra pressure on top of his head. He knew someone was above him. He fought to keep from fainting.

The garage men hurried over.

"Send for the police. There's a firebox down the street," Whittaker called.

Tommy Whittaker began to dig. He uncovered a wrist watch. He thought he recognized the watchband. He kept digging, until he uncovered the man's side. He saw the man was still breathing, but his respiration was very weak.

Then Tommy Whittaker recognized my brother, but by then Jack had fainted. Whittaker dug more frantically.

The rescue squad arrived. They applied an oxygen mask to Jack while they were still digging him out. From busy Washington Street, a crowd gathered.

Jack revived slightly when they put him on a stretcher. It was 6:30 P.M. He spied Tommy Whittaker.

"Who found me?" he asked.

"I did," said Whittaker.

With his lips, Jack formed one word.

"Thanks."

There was no more powerful word.

TWENTY-FIVE

"Don't Let It End This Way"

BY SUE KIDD
ANDERSON, SOUTH CAROLINA

A Father's Day story to touch your heart.
Always remember: The time to love is short.

The hospital was unusually quiet that bleak January evening, quiet and still, like the air before a storm. I stood in the nurses' station on the seventh floor and glanced at the clock. It was 9:00 P.M.

I threw a stethoscope around my neck and headed for room 712, last room on the hall. Room 712 had a new patient, Mr. Williams. A man all alone. A man strangely silent about his family.

As I entered the room, Mr. Williams looked up eagerly, but dropped his eyes when he saw it was only I, his nurse. I pressed the stethoscope over his chest and listened. Strong, slow, even beating. Just what I wanted to hear. There seemed little indication he had suffered a slight heart attack a few hours earlier.

He looked up from his starched white bed. "Nurse, would you . . ." He hesitated, tears filling his eyes. Once before he had started to ask me a question, but had changed his mind.

I touched his hand, waiting.

He brushed away a tear. "Would you call my daughter? Tell her I've had a heart attack. A slight one. You see, I live alone and she is the only family I have." His respiration suddenly speeded up.

I turned his nasal oxygen up to eight liters a minute. "Of course, I'll call her," I said, studying his face.

He gripped the sheets and pulled himself forward, his face tense with urgency. "Will you call her right away—as soon as you can?" He was breathing fast—too fast.

"I'll call her the very first thing," I said, patting his shoulder. "Now you get some rest."

I flipped off the light. He closed his eyes, such young blue eyes in his fifty-year-old face.

Room 712 was dark except for a faint night-light under the sink. Oxygen gurgled in the green tubes above his bed. Reluctant to leave, I moved through the shadowy silence to the window. The panes were cold. Below a foggy mist curled through the hospital parking lot. Above snow clouds quilted the night sky. I shivered.

"Nurse," he called. "Could you get me a pencil and paper?"

I dug a scrap of yellow paper and a pen from my pocket and set it on the bedside table.

"Thank you," he said.

I smiled at him and left.

I walked back to the nurses' station and sat in a squeaky swivel chair by the phone. Mr. William's daughter was listed on his chart as the next of kin. I got her number from information and dialed. Her soft voice answered.

"Janie, this is Sue Kidd, a registered nurse at the hospital. I'm calling about your father. He was admitted today with a slight heart attack and . . ."

"No!" she screamed into the phone, startling me. "He's not dying is he?" It was more a painful plea than a question.

"His condition is stable at the moment," I said, trying hard to sound convincing.

Silence. I bit my lip.

"You must not let him die!" she said. Her voice was so utterly compelling that my hand trembled on the phone.

"He is getting the very best care."

"But you don't understand," she pleaded. "My daddy and I haven't spoken in almost a year. We had a terrible argument on my twenty-first birthday, over my boyfriend. I ran out of the house. I . . . I haven't been back. All these months I've wanted to go to him for forgiveness. The last thing I said to him was, 'I hate you.'"

Her voice cracked and I heard her heave great agonizing sobs. I sat, listening, tears burning my eyes. A father and a daughter, so lost to each other! Then I was thinking of my own father, many miles away. It had been so long since I had said I love you.

As Janie struggled to control her tears, I breathed a prayer. "Please God, let this daughter find forgiveness."

"I'm coming, now! I'll be there in thirty minutes," she said. *Click.* She had hung up.

I tried to busy myself with a stack of charts on the desk. I couldn't concentrate. Room 712. I knew I had to get back to 712. I hurried down the hall nearly in a run. I opened the door.

Mr. Williams lay unmoving. I reached for his pulse. There was none.

"Code ninety-nine. Room 712. Code ninety-nine. Stat." The alert was shooting through the hospital within seconds after I called the switchboard through the intercom by the bed.

Mr. Williams had had a cardiac arrest.

With lightning speed I leveled the bed and bent over his mouth, breathing air into his lungs. I positioned my head over his chest and compressed. One, two, three. I tried to count. At fifteen, I moved back to his mouth and breathed as deeply as I could. Where was help? Again I compressed and breathed. Compressed and breathed. He could not die!

"Oh, God," I prayed. "His daughter is coming. Don't let it end this way."

The door burst open. Doctors and nurses poured into the room, pushing emergency equipment. A doctor took over the manual compression of the heart. A tube was inserted through his mouth as an airway. Nurses plunged syringes of medicine into the intravenous tubing.

I connected the heart monitor. Nothing. Not a beat. My own heart pounded. "God, don't let it end like this. Not in bitterness and hatred. His daughter is coming. Let her find peace."

"Stand back," cried a doctor. I handed him the paddles for the electrical shock to the heart. He placed them on Mr. William's chest.

Over and over we tried. But nothing. No response. Mr. Williams was dead.

A nurse unplugged the oxygen. The gurgling stopped. One by one they left, grim and silent.

How could this happen? How? I stood by his bed, stunned. A cold wind rattled the window, pelting the panes with snow. Outside—everywhere—seemed a bed of blackness, cold and dark. How could I face his daughter?

When I left the room, I saw her against the wall by a water fountain. A doctor, who had been in 712 only moments before, stood at her side, talking to her, gripping her elbow. Then he moved on, leaving her slumped against the wall.

Such pathetic hurt reflected from her face. Such wounded eyes. She knew. The doctor had told her her father was gone.

I took her hand and led her into the nurses' lounge. We sat on little green stools, neither saying a word. She stared straight ahead at a pharmaceutical calendar, glass-faced, almost breakable-looking.

"Janie, I'm so, so sorry," I said. It was pitifully inadequate.

"I never hated him, you know. I loved him," she said.

God, please help her, I prayed.

Suddenly she whirled toward me. "I want to see him."

My first thought was, *Why put yourself through more pain? Seeing him will only make it worse.* But I got up and wrapped my arm around her. We walked slowly down the corridor to 712. Outside the door I squeezed her hand, wishing she would change her mind about going inside. She pushed open the door.

We moved to the bed, huddled together, taking small steps in unison, Janie leaned over the bed and buried her face in the sheets.

I tried not to look at her, at this sad, sad good-bye. I backed against the bedside table. My hand fell upon a scrap of yellow paper. I picked it up. I read.

My dearest Janie, I forgive you. I pray you will also forgive me. I know that you love me. I love you, too. Daddy.

The note was shaking in my hands as I thrust it toward Janie. She read it once. Then twice. Her tormented face grew radiant. Peace began to glisten in her eyes. She hugged the scrap of paper to her breast.

"Thank you, God," I whispered, looking up at the window. A few crystal stars blinked through the blackness. A snowflake hit the window and melted away, gone forever.

Life seemed as fragile as a snowflake on the window. But thank you, God, the relationships, sometimes fragile as snowflakes, can be mended together again. But there is not a moment to spare.

I crept from the room and hurried to the phone. I would call my own father. I would say, "I love you."

TWENTY-SIX

Nowhere Else to Go

BY DONNIE GALLOWAY
GOLD HILL, NORTH CAROLINA

A five-ton truck hauling eleven tons of bricks. A crowded bridge. A sudden stop . . .

Mile after lonely mile, I kept thinking of my cousin. The thoughts were submerged, hidden down deep, and I tried not to pay them any mind. I talked to other truckers on my CB some, read all the signs for Hackey's and Fieldcrest and furniture outlets posted on U.S. Interstate 85. I stopped off for a bite to eat at Darrell's Barbecue in Rockwell, North Carolina.

But, like a magnet, my mind kept coming back to my cousin. We had been close, he and I. Two weeks before, he had killed himself. His suicide stunned me, and inside I felt a heaviness, like a weight, tight, in my chest.

Sad and puzzled, I thought back to some of those times we hung around together. We had talked for hours about this or that. He was young. Life was before him, but . . .

Death. We had never talked about that. It had been raining off and on, and the grayness of the day seemed to play on my mind. I was driving south, hauling a load of bricks from Lewis Run, Pennsylvania, to Baton Rouge, Louisiana. It was 1982, and I had been running heavy freight for ten years, ever since I was eighteen.

As the 1972 Brockway truck and I pushed into my home territory of North Carolina, those thoughts of death traveled with me. I remembered grimly that I hadn't even been able to go to his funeral. My mother had to tell me about it. The company I drove for then wouldn't let me off even though I had been asked to be a pallbearer.

It was sprinkling as I pulled out of the weigh station south of Charlotte. I was about to undergo a great change. If only my cousin had still been alive and riding with me that day. His life might have changed, just as mine did.

Just ahead was the Catawba River Bridge, a span of 175 yards. As I drove onto the bridge, an orange sign announced: Right Lane Closed—1000 Feet Ahead.

I waited for a lady in a small car to pass, then I pulled over into the left lane behind her.

Suddenly, right in front of me, all of the cars had stopped. But I couldn't! Five tons of metal and eleven tons of bricks were going to smash right into all those people.

Oh no, dear God, I'm going to kill all of them! my mind screamed. *There's nowhere else to go,* I thought desperately, pulling the wheel hard to the right.

In a split second, I knew I had to drive off the bridge. It was either that or kill everyone in front of me.

As I swerved and drove to the edge of the bridge, I heard metal crash into metal. Then I was through the guardrail and falling. . . .

The truck and the bricks and I plunged eighty feet through the air. I was terrified. *This is it!*

We hit the river hard, and the windshield burst. Muddy water gushed in and swept me back into the sleeper. The truck sank thirty-five feet to the river bottom in a hurry. I was dazed, and my sleeping gear and tools and everything I owned floated around me, confusing me. I couldn't see.

I groped through the blackness. My clothes and boots felt like lead. My lungs were about to burst. I would never get out of there alive.

I touched the steering wheel. Beyond was the open windshield and I struggled to it just as the truck began flipping over in a slow arc. Soon my opening would be lying against the river bottom, and I would be trapped.

I kicked and pushed, pulling myself through. But then, I was lost. I felt as if I were in a tomb, surrounded by choking blackness. Which way was up? I didn't know. I just stretched out my arms and swam.

My head hit the river bottom. That is when I gave up. I did say some prayers, but it was my time to die.

"Dear God, if you want me to live or if you want me to die, please go with me. And, dear God, help those people on the bridge. Don't let anyone be hurt, please."

I gave up to whatever was going to happen. And I didn't feel afraid anymore.

Then I felt my body lifting up . . . *and up and up*—ten feet, twenty, thirty, thirty-five. I was being pushed up. I broke onto the surface, and there was a boat with two fishermen motoring toward me!

I gasped and choked and hollered and went under a couple of times, but I fought my way back to the top. I was still alive! I fought to stay afloat until those fishermen grabbed me and pulled me into their boat.

I lay on the bottom of the boat gasping and coughing, gulping in small breaths of air. It felt good, breathing in life again.

Then I managed to say, "Did I hurt anyone? Is everyone OK?"

We looked up at the bridge deck. There were flashing lights. Troopers and wreckers. Crowds of people looking down at us. I gulped. There was an ambulance. *Somebody must have gotten hurt bad,* I thought. For just a second, living didn't feel so good anymore.

The two men with me in the boat propelled up to the bridge, asking if anyone else was hurt. Then I heard the answering voice, "Everybody's OK up here. We called an ambulance for the trucker."

"How is the trucker?" someone shouted from the bridge.

"A bit winded, but he's in pretty good shape!"

Good shape. Well, one of my legs may never be the same, and my back gives me some trouble now, but I'm still hauling heavy loads on an eighteen-wheeler flatbed truck. And I still drive sometimes over the Catawba River Bridge. There is a patch in the guardrail where I drove through that day, and that patch reminds me of the lesson I learned down on the bottom of that river. I learned something special about life.

I learned it while I was facing death. I knew down there that I would never be afraid of death, but I also discovered something else, something that my cousin could have learned, but didn't. You don't need to be afraid of *life,* either. Because if you will just reach out and ask God to go with you, he'll lift you up and walk with you the rest of the way.

God has a purpose for each one of us. He wants us to live, and he will give us the courage to live, if we just give him the chance.

TWENTY-SEVEN

The Waterman

BY LEON LEWIS
HOOPERSVILLE, MARYLAND
AS TOLD TO JOHN SHERRILL

It's a life of uncertainty, danger—and beauty.

As I steer my fishing boat out of Tyler's Cove into Chesapeake Bay this early morning, I glance back through the wheelhouse window. There in the stern of the *Agnes Elizabeth* is my son, Lemuel, thirty-five now, sitting on an upended bushel basket, sharpening his knife. Standing near him is his son, Stephen, eleven and rawboned like his dad. Stephen is out with us just for the day. He is peering through the mist to see the sun come up over the Maryland shore.

Three generations of Lewises on board. And nobody knows how many Lewis fathers and sons before us have worked here on the bay, oystering and crabbing and fishing, since the family came over from England three hundred years ago.

As I clear the cove, heading for our nets an hour away, young Stephen appears at the wheelhouse door, not saying anything, just waiting, as his father and his uncles had waited when they were eleven years old.

"All right, Steve," I say, "take the wheel."

Steve must have had his fish basket ready on the deck just outside. In no time he has it upside down behind the wheel and is standing on it, scanning the water ahead. I don't have to tell him to keep the red channel markers to port. I wave to a crabber, out checking his pots. With Steve at the wheel the boat plows steadily along and I settle back. . . .

Some people might wonder why we Lewises keep coming onto the water. Why do we get up at four in the morning, knowing we might not get back until eleven at night? Why do we put up with the uncertainty, never knowing what the catch will be or what the market will bring? Or the danger? The Chesapeake can be as violent as it is beautiful. One of my brothers was drowned here. I have had a boat sink under me when I hit a submerged object. And out there to port I can see where our firstborn, Bud, Lemuel's older brother, went down when he was just twenty years old.

But here we are, more than two decades later, Lem and Steve and I, out on this same water. I watch as young Stephen maneuvers around a buoy in the shallower water near our pound nets on the western shore. A short way off, a fish hawk is screaming from her nest on top of a piling. I watch the boy smile up at the bird and I think, *It's happening again. Here's a new generation of watermen finding some private, secret satisfaction on the bay.*

"I'll take it now, Steve," I say.

Stephen jumps off his basket and runs out to the deck to peer down into the net as we draw alongside. Fishing with a pound net is an old Indian trick. Stretching out from shore for almost five hundred yards is a line of pine poles that we had cut and driven into the mud of the bay. Tied to the poles is a long, tapering net that guides fish into smaller and smaller heart-shaped pounds, until they reach the last one, the pocket. Every day except Sunday we come here to harvest our catch.

I tie up outside the net and join Steve and his father on deck. We can't see what the pocket holds. One thing about fishing, you never know what is going to be in your net. Sometimes there is almost nothing and you don't meet expenses. But if the blues or alewives are running, that pocket can hold thousands of fish. Steve laughs as a cormorant surfaces from within the net and tries to fly off. That old bird is so stuffed he can barely flop away.

"I bet he's been gorging on blues, Poppop!" Steve says to me.

If Steve is right, there will be a good harvest today. The blue can be three feet long, and he usually travels in schools. That fish is lots of mischief. His teeth are rows of razors, and he snaps at anything that moves. When he is in a feeding frenzy he will cut and tear and slash, and then force up what is in his belly so he can go on gorging.

Lemuel now unties the skiff. We tow it behind the *Agnes Elizabeth* and he rows it over the top rim of the net until he is inside the pocket. Lemuel reaches down with a hook, grabs one strand of net and manhandles it up into the skiff. Over and over Lemuel bunts the net, shrinking the diameter until the fish are drawn close to the side of the *Agnes Elizabeth.* Now I can see thousands of fish flashing in the morning sun. I make out a few yellow-fin trout and jellyfish, but mostly—as Steve had guessed—blues.

I start up the hydraulic spool that powers the huge bailing net we use to haul our catch aboard. With the spool whining, I plunge the bailer into the rolling water, then swing it up and over the waist. I pull the drawstring, and a river of fish smelling of saltwater thuds aboard. The boy and I wade up to the top of our boots through leaping, thrashing fish, picking them up with thick gloves and tossing them into the baskets.

An hour passes and Lemuel climbs aboard. It is time to head home.

As we start back the thought returns. *What is it that pulls Lewis men and boys to the water?* Part of the draw is the generations themselves, father and son working together. I was on the water when I was still in grade school, setting a trotline weekends or dredging for oysters on my father's bugeye when we still worked under sail. The older men taught us to respect the water, knowing the risks, but knowing the riches too.

The riches had nothing to do with cash in the bank. We never had much money when I was a boy, but there was always fish to eat, and you could grow things and go hunting. I remember the platters my mother put on the table, rounded off with oysters and crab cakes and black duck, served up with corn and beans and tomatoes from her garden.

But the sea is more than the living it provides. It is in the blood. It's a relationship with the Lord. Out here on the water God is closer to you. You can come to know him. Really know him, I mean, not just visit him once a week. I know this because I've heard him. Heard him out there.

There, off to starboard now, is the spot where our boy drowned.

Bud went down just four months after he became a father. But he died doing what he always wanted to do. I can't remember a time when Bud hadn't wanted to be on the bay. He built four boats before he was out of high school, though the one that went down was the bigger commercial fisher. I helped Bud finance that boat. He had her loaded with the latest safety gear—depth finder, auxiliary pump, ship-to-ship radio, all designed to help in the bay's hard blows and sudden fogs.

Bud's boat wasn't lost in a storm or fog. She exploded. We had gasoline engines instead of diesel back in the early sixties, and the way we figured it later, there could have been a leak in the fuel pump, letting fumes build up in the bilge. One spark from a loose plug was all it would take after that. Bud had a crew of two with him that morning—his brother Lemuel, twelve at the time and skinny as a needlefish, and Bud's friend Arvie. The explosion threw Arvie into the water. Bud and Lem tried to reach the life preservers, but the flames were too hot, so they threw empty gas cans into the water and jumped overboard. They got a can to Arvie, who was almost unconscious. For a while the three huddled together, praying.

"Lem, my time has come."

Bud nodded toward Arvie, whose leaky can had begun to sink.

"Lem," Bud went on, "you're lighter than Arvie. How 'bout you swap cans with him?"

So young Lemuel gave the older boy his gasoline can. Our son Bud stayed afloat just a few minutes longer, then went down. In a moment his friend Arvie followed. When help finally came, little Lemuel was nearly gone too.

When Lemuel, badly burned, was brought ashore by a crabber, my wife, Rosa, raced him to the hospital while I got equipment to drag the bay for the boys' bodies. About thirty fishing boat captains from all over the bay showed up to help find Bud and Arvie. I appreciated that, but I wanted to find my boy myself, without help from anybody. Up until then I thought anything there was to do, I could do it. Alone.

We found Arvie early the next day but it looked like we weren't going to find Bud. For two more hours the flotilla of fishing boats crisscrossed the bay. I took one of the boats that Bud himself had built and went back and forth, back and forth, always asking God to let me be the one to find my boy.

"Do you have to do it by yourself?"

The voice was as clear as that and I knew I had just heard the Lord speak.

There is a time, he was saying, when it's right to be self-reliant, and there's a time to give up trying to do everything yourself. Did I have to find Bud with no one helping?

"No," I said, very softly. "Just as long as we find him, Lord, I don't have to do it alone anymore."

At that very moment one of the men in another boat hooked onto a piece of Bud's clothing. They brought our boy to the surface, and I sailed over to bring him in. I never in my life wanted more to take him in my arms, not even when he was a baby. I laid Bud on the deck and brought him back in the boat he built.

After that day, nothing was ever the same for me. I had learned that the most resourceful man in the world isn't as big as the bay. Out on the bay I had learned how small I was.

Up ahead now is Tyler's Cove. I can see our truck coming down the road with Rosa at the wheel. She'll drive with me to the market up in Cambridge. Lem and Steve have finished sorting the catch, and Steve's standing in the bow watching a heron stalk the shore. The bird stabs his beak into the water and comes up with a fish. The old heron will never get rich any more than we will, but the look in his eye says he is doing what he was designed to do.

That is what helped me and Rosa and Bud's widow most—to know that Bud had been doing the thing he most wanted to do.

And isn't that why we Lewises come onto the water generation after generation? It's a living, yes, but it's a lot more than that. There's pain, but there's a kind of completion too. Men don't stay on the bay unless they are built for the life. Like that old heron. Like Bud.

And like young Steve? As we pull up to the wharf at Tyler's Cove and Lem jumps onto the dock, Steve tosses him a line, and then the boy turns toward me and comes out with the question I knew he would be asking me one day.

"Poppop," Steve asks, very serious, "this summer when school's out, would you be needing a boy on board?"

I put my hand on the lad's shoulder and we step off the gently swaying *Agnes Elizabeth* onto the dock where his grandmother is waiting.

"Well, I might, Steve," I say. "If he's a hard-working boy."

TWENTY-EIGHT

Out of the Sky

BY STEVE DAVIS
DALLAS, TEXAS

It's still shrouded in mystery—but what a beautiful mystery—the day the plane dropped out of the sky.

Visibility was less than marginal the afternoon of November 17, 1976. Not one of us sitting around the flight business office at Hunt's Airport in Portland, Texas, would have bet more than a dollar that a plane could get through to land. No one counted on the little Cessna 172 that came barreling out of a sky as dark and choppy as lentil soup. And I couldn't have imagined how it would change my life forever.

I had awakened that morning feeling pretty pleased with myself. One year before, when I had arrived from North Carolina, my life savings easily fit into my pocket. But now, at twenty-three, I had it made—or so I thought. I was a flight instructor with my own thriving flight school and three airplanes of my own. One of my first Texas students had been a beautiful young woman named Linda Peters, who was now my girlfriend. I had more money than I needed. That day I was so self-satisfied that I didn't even mind that it was too cold and rainy to do any flight instructing. "Northerns" often hit southern

Texas, but they blow on through within a couple of days.

Bad weather for flight instructing is perfect weather for indulging in a little "hangar flying." So I pulled on my bomber jacket and drove over to the Chicken Shack to pick up lunch for the boys: Jess, the retiree who did our books; Ray; and A.A., who in his sixties, was finally learning to fly. By the time I got back it was drizzling and so foggy I couldn't even make out Corpus Christi across the bay. Only instrument-rated pilots could fly in this weather, and they would have to fly into the bigger, tower-controlled Corpus Christi International.

But inside, the atmosphere was convivial. I put out the chicken, and we all sat round on the fraying vinyl furniture and jawed a bit, telling tall tales and patching the world's woes. Jess and Ray went on ribbing A.A. for taking up flying so late in life.

"Well, better late than never," A.A. said. "Not like Steve. To hear him tell it, he could fly before he could walk."

"That's right," I agreed. "My mom and dad said the only time I would sit still was in an airplane with them." And I told them how I had spent most of my childhood in Mexico, where my dad had been a missionary pilot. As I talked I could see myself as a ten-year-old in shirt sleeves, riding along dusty roads with my dad to the airstrip outside of Guadalajara. How often I had pictured turning the corner and rumbling up to the most beautiful sight in the world—our Fairchild 24. A hunk of junk, really, an old tail-dragger my dad bought for $300. He had hung a radial engine in it—an old round one with lots of horsepower. Nice and noisy.

"Let's load 'er up, Steve!" Dad would call, and we would put in as many crates of supplies as the plane could carry. Then we would strap in. There wasn't a takeoff that didn't scare—and thrill—me to the bottom of my sandals. Then we would be up in the open skies, flying over villages and rain forests and mountain ranges.

"I think I'll take a few winks, Steve. Hold 'er steady," Dad would say, and he would doze off—or pretend to—while I had held course and altitude. Then he would set her down in some mountaintop village that had been waiting for the supplies we were bringing.

The guys grunted their appreciation of the scene and I quit talking. But there was something there, in my past, that was gnawing at me, and had been for the past few months. As the others went on talking, I mentally stayed behind in that mountaintop village.

After we unloaded the supplies, Dad would gather the natives around, and tell them about *Jesucristo, El Salvador.* I soaked up every word. Jesus Christ had been intensely real to me then. I even thought of myself as a missionary, and all I wanted to do was to grow up and be a man like Nate Saint, a pilot I had read about in a book my parents had given me. The book was *Through Gates of Splendor* by Elisabeth Elliot. It was the story of five missionaries, including Mrs. Elliot's husband, who were martyred by Indians in Ecuador in 1956. It was a moving story of faith and adventure, but the part I almost committed to memory was about my hero, Nate Saint, the young pilot who flew them on their missions. I admired him so much that when I held course for my dad, I'd imagine I *was* Nate Saint, flying much-needed supplies to remote corners of the jungle. Soon, it *would* be me!

Just the memory of that time brought a catch to my throat. I'd been so joyful, so confident of God. I had had a faith like Nate Saint's, worth risking everything for. But somewhere along the line . . . what had happened to it? I lived in the adult world now, a world of doubts and conflicts and temptations. Since there was no one around to help me deal with these nagging doubts, I found it much easier to ignore them. So I had quit worrying about Christianity and devoted all my attention to flying. But where my faith once had been, there was now a profound sense of loss. I felt empty inside.

Recently I had come across my old copy of *Through Gates of Splendor.* I had tried to put the book away, but I couldn't shake the sadness that gripped me—because of Nate's death, because of my own loss of faith. Finally I stopped and said the first prayer I had said in years: "Now, wait a minute, God. Something tells me you're not real. I'd really like to know you the way I thought I did. I want to have the faith I used to have. But I just can't blindly accept that stuff I grew up with. If you'll let me know that you're real, I will serve you, but I've got to know. I can't pretend."

I didn't feel any answer to my prayer. In fact, I didn't feel anything at all. And that made me angry.

No, I'd thought. *It's all a farce. My boyhood hero, Nate Saint, wasted his life. He died for nothing.*

The book had fallen open to the photo section, and I had looked at the picture of Nate's son, Steve, then five years old. *That kid would probably be about my age now,* I figured. *And if the truth be known, he is probably in worse shape spiritually today than I am.*

In disgust and anger I had put the book away. Now, sitting in the flight business office on this stormy day, I was still angry.

I tried to shake those thoughts and get back into the conversation. Wouldn't the guys laugh if they knew I had been asking for proof from a nonexistent God—and that I was all torn up because no answer was forthcoming?

"Wa-a-ll, we might as well close up," said Jess. "The rain's only getting worse."

As we all stood to start closing, Julio, one of Mr. Hunt's workers, stopped in. He liked to talk with me because I was one of the few folks around who was fluent in Spanish, his native tongue.

"Hola, Steve," he said. *"Aquí viene un avión loco."*

We looked out through the rain, and sure enough, a little Cessna 172 was dropping out of the sky toward the airstrip.

"Nice day for a little scud-running," laughed A.A. But we all breathed a sigh of relief when the plane touched down safely and taxied in.

"Probably drug runners," decided Ray. "What other business would have you out flying on a day like this?"

A few minutes later the pilot and the passenger swung the door open and came in, dripping. They were both young and clean-cut.

"Hello," the pilot started. "We barely made it in. I'm not instrument rated—I didn't think I was going to find an uncontrolled airport. Can we tie down? Is there a motel in town where we can stay and wait for better weather?"

"We're just closing," said Jess. "But yeah, you can tie down." A.A. and Ray were already heading out.

"There's a motel in Portland," I said. "If you hurry up, I'll wait and drive you over." I turned back to Julio to continue our conversation about the weather. *"Este tiempo está malo."*

"Y peligroso también," agreed the pilot. *"Yo no debía haber volado el avión con un día còmo éste* [I had no business flying on a day like this]."

The three of us had talked for a few minutes before I realized how odd it was that the pilot, a blond, blue-eyed Anglo, was speaking fluent Spanish.

"Where'd you learn the language?" I asked.

"My parents were missionaries in Ecuador," he said. "I grew up there."

"Really?" I asked. "Did you ever hear of any of those missionaries who were martyred down there twenty years ago?"

"One of them was his dad," the passenger said.

"Oh, yeah?" I pursued. "What's your name?"

"Steve Saint," he said.

The boy from the book!

All the air went out of me, like I had been punched in the chest. It was as if God had used that book to kindle my faith as a child, and now, when I had deeper questions, the boy in the book flew out of its pages and stood here before me!

But did he have any faith? Or was this a cruel coincidence?

It was minutes before I found my voice, but when I did, I tried to act nonchalant. "If you guys want to save your motel bill, I live a mile from here. There's a couch you could stay on tonight."

"That would be great," said Steve.

Far into the night I talked with Steve and his friend, Jim. I wanted to find out what had happened to Steve—did he still believe in God?

When I discovered he had a strong relationship with God and that his father's death had *strengthened* his faith, I grilled him mercilessly. Not once did I mention the book or my childhood. Instead, all of my questioning and anger spewed out toward Nate Saint's son. And he quietly answered each accusation with faith. The relief I felt at letting all of this out was enormous. After all these years I could finally express my doubts, because Steve Saint had a God big enough and real enough to handle them.

The next day the weather cleared. I stood alone on the runway after Steve and Jim took off. Everything at Hunt's Airport was the same—except me. Twenty-four hours after that physical—and spiritual—storm, I knew that God had answered my prayer in the most personal, loving way possible. Again I had a joy inside that even an airplane had never been able to produce.

There has been a change in Linda's life too. She also has a close relationship with Christ. We have been married for almost ten years now and have flown many missions to remote, impoverished villages in Mexico and Central America. But as long as I live, I'll never forget that November day after Steve Saint took off, when I gazed again into the sky—the sky my prayer had sailed through, the sky my dad and Nate Saint and I had flown through, the sky out of which that little Cessna had come barreling. And I knew that through that sky over the horizon in Mexico and Central America, hungry villages waited for someone like Nate Saint—or me—to fly in with food, and a faith worth risking everything for. And, thanks to God, the faith again was mine.

TWENTY-NINE

I Saw the Hand of God Move

BY JOE STEVENSON
RENO, NEVADA

A father and his son. The story of a long, rough road to faith.

I have always believed in God. But over the years my beliefs about who God is—and what he can do—have changed. It wasn't until my son was gravely ill that I learned you can believe in God and yet not know him at all.

Know. Knowledge. Logic. When I was younger, those were the words I wanted to live by. As a child, I contracted scarlet fever, and this illness ruled out my ever playing sports or roughhousing around. The only real adventures I could go on were adventures of the mind. I read books with a vengeance—Great Books of the Western World, and the volumes of Will and Ariel Durant, and literally thousands more—and out of my reading I formed my strongest beliefs. I believed in logic, in the mind's ability to put all creation into neat, rational categories.

At the same time, I was growing up in a strongly Christian family, and so I believed in God. But I insisted—and my insistence caused a lot of arguments—that God himself was also a Being bound by logic and his own natural laws. I guess I pictured God as a great scientist. Miracles? No, God couldn't and wouldn't break laws in that way. When my family told me that Christianity means faith in a loving, miraculous God, I turned away and went looking for other religions—ones that respected the rational mind above all.

As I became a man, my belief in rationality helped me in my career. I became a salesman for the Bell System, and when I needed to formulate sales strategies and targets, logic unlocked a lot of doors on the way to success.

But other doors seemed to be closed. I felt dry, spiritually empty, and anxious. I tried meditation, E.S.P., and so on, but the emptiness increased to despair.

In utter defeat, I turned to God in prayer. His Spirit answered with, "I don't simply want belief that I exist. I want you, your will, your life, your dreams, your goals, your very being. And I want your faith, faith that I am sufficient for all your needs." My despair overcame my logic and I yielded all to him. But just saying you have faith is not the same as having it. In my mind, I still had God in a box.

Maybe that was why I never thought to pray when my oldest son Frank came home from first grade one day and said he didn't feel well. What would God care about stomach flu?

A doctor whom my wife Janice and I had consulted wasn't very alarmed about Frank's illness at first. "It's really not too serious," the doctor assured us, "Just a bad case of the flu complicated by a little acidosis. Give him this medicine and in a few days he will be fine."

But Frank wasn't fine—not at all. The medicine worked for a day or so, but then his symptoms—the gagging, choking, and vomiting—came back more violently. His small, six-year-old frame was bathed in sweat and racked with convulsions. We checked him into the local hospital for further testing, but later in the evening, our doctor said the original diagnosis was correct. "He's just got a real bad case of it," we were told.

I went to work the next day fully expecting to take Frank and Janice home that night, but when I stopped at the hospital to pick them up, our doctor was there to meet me.

"I'd like to have a word with you two," he said, showing Janice and me into a private room.

"A problem, Doctor?" I asked.

"Further testing has shown our previous diagnosis was incorrect. We think your son has acute nephritis. It's a terminal kidney disease. . . ." He paused, and I could feel the blood running from my face. "But we've found that in children there's a good chance of recovery. Your son has a 90 percent chance of being as good as new."

But by ten o'clock the next morning, the news was worse. Sometime during the night, Frank's kidneys had failed. Janice and I rushed to the hospital again.

"X rays show Frank's kidneys are so badly infected that no fluid will pass through them," we were told. "The odds aren't in his favor anymore. If those kidneys don't start working within forty-eight hours, I'm afraid your son will die."

I looked at Janice, watching the tears well in her eyes as a huge lump formed in my throat. I took her hand in mine and slowly we walked back to Frank's room. We were too shocked, too upset to even talk. All afternoon we sat at Frank's bedside, watching, stroking his matted blond hair, wiping his damp forehead. The stillness of the room was broken only by the beeps and blips of the machines monitoring little Frank's condition. Specialists would occasionally come, adjust a few tubes, make some marks on Frank's chart, and then silently go. I searched their eyes for an answer, for some glimmer of hope, and got nothing. When our minister came to pray for our son, I could only cry in desperation.

Late that evening, after Frank was asleep, we went home. Friends were waiting with a hot meal, words of encouragement, and news of a vast prayer chain they had begun. And for a fleeting moment, I thought I saw in Janice's eyes the spark of hope that I had been looking for from the doctors all afternoon.

By the following morning, that spark of hope had ignited a flame of confidence in Janice. "I turned Frank's life over to God last night," she told me excitedly, before we were even out of bed. "I feel a real peace about what's going to happen, that God's will is going to be done."

"God's will?" I said angrily. "What kind of God makes little boys get sick? He doesn't care!" And I rolled over. Peace? God's will? No, little Frank would need more than that to get well!

But my anger didn't stop me from trying to reason with God. All that morning, while Janice kept a hospital vigil, I begged and pleaded and screamed at God, daring him to disprove my skepticism, trying to goad him into action.

"Who do you think you are?" I shouted once. "Why are you doing this to my son? He's only six! Everybody says you're such a loving

God—why don't you show it?" I yelled until I was exhausted. Finally, convinced my arguments were falling on deaf ears, I took our other children to a neighbor and headed to the hospital, thinking this might be the last time I would see my son alive.

I never arrived. At least, a part of me didn't. In the car on the way, this Higher Being, this remote Power, this "unjust" God, spoke to me through his Spirit. I felt his presence, soothing my still-hot anger. And I heard his voice, gentle, reassuring. He reminded me that I had made a commitment to him, that I had promised to trust him with my life, my all. And he had promised to take care of me, in all circumstances. *Take me out of the box you've put me in,* he said, *and let me work.*

By the time I parked the car, my heart was beating wildly. I sat for a few moments longer, and uttered but two words in reply to all that had happened: "Forgive me."

By the time I reached Frank's room, I knew what I needed to do as clearly as if someone had given me written instructions. There had been no change in Frank's condition, so I sent Janice home to get some rest. Then I walked over to Frank's bed. Placing shaking hands on where I thought his kidneys should be, I prayed as I never believed I would ever pray. "God, forgive me for my ego, for trying to make you what I want you to be. If you will, heal my son, and if you won't, that's all right, too. I'll trust you. But, please, do either right now, I pray in Christ's name. Amen."

That was all. There were no lightning flashes, no glows, no surges of emotion like the rushing wind, only the *blip-blip-blip* of monitors. I calmly sat down in a chair, picked up a magazine, and began to wait for God's answer. There was only one difference. For the first time in my life, I knew I was going to get one.

Within moments my eyes were drawn from the magazine to a catheter tube leading from Frank's frail-looking body. That tube was supposed to drain fluid from his kidneys, but for nearly two days it had been perfectly dry, meaning Frank's kidneys weren't working at all. But when I looked closely at the top of the tube, I saw a small drop of clear fluid forming. Ever so slowly it expanded, like a drop of water forming on the head of a leaky faucet, until it became heavy enough to run down the tube and into the collecting jar.

This was the most wonderful thing I had ever seen—the hand of God, working. I watched the tube, transfixed, fully expecting to see another drop of fluid form. In about two minutes, I did. Soon, the drops were coming regularly, about a minute apart. With every drip, I could hear God saying to me, *I am and I care.*

When the nurse came in on her regular half-hour rounds, she could barely contain her excitement. "Do you see this, do you see this?" she shouted, pointing to the collecting jar. "Do you know that this is more fluid than your son has secreted in the past forty-eight hours combined?" She grabbed the catheter and raised it, saying she wanted to get every drop, then rushed off.

Within minutes she was back. Grabbing a chair, she sat down next to me and, excitedly, we watched drops of fluid run down the tube. We were both awed at what was happening. For half an hour we murmured only short sentences. "Isn't God good?" she asked me once, and I nodded. When she finally got up to call the doctor, I went to call Janice.

An hour and a half later one of the specialists assigned to Frank's case arrived. Taking one look at the collector, he told us that it was a false alarm, that the fluid was too clear. Anything coming from a kidney as infected as Frank's was would be rust-colored and filled with pus. No, he said, the fluid had to be coming from somewhere else. But I knew—Frank was well again.

By the next morning, more than 500 centimeters of the clear fluid had passed into the collector, and it continued as the doctors ran tests and X rays to try to determine its origin. Finally, two days later, our doctor called us into his office.

"Joe, Janice, I think we've been privileged to witness an act of God. All the X rays taken in the last two days not only show no kidney infection, they show no sign that there was even an infection. Frank's blood pressure and blood poison levels have also dropped suddenly. This is a definite miracle."

And this time I wasn't about to argue. At last I fully believed in a God whose love knows no bounds—not the bounds of logic, not the hold of natural laws.

Faith. That's what I now had . . . that and the knowledge that one's belief in God is essentially hollow if the belief isn't founded on faith.

THIRTY

Aboard the San Francisco Zephyr

BY SALLY TROUTMAN
ETHEL, MISSOURI

A flood, a crash, a friend, a prayer—all on my first time away from home alone.

It was after midnight when the San Francisco Zephyr—a twelve-car superliner from Chicago—pulled out of the station in Ottumwa, Iowa. I didn't even try to hold back my tears as I waved good-bye to Mom and Dad. I was their baby, the youngest of four, and I had never been away from home by myself before.

I was glad about my summer job—counselor for a month at a Camp Fire Girls camp near Lake Tahoe in Nevada. But I felt nervous and unsure—about everything. Could I get along on my own—much less supervise others?

The train picked up speed. I leaned against the window and swallowed hard. Back home my parents would find the Father's Day card I had left for Dad.

"Thank you for letting me go," a note on it said. "Whatever happens, please don't ever regret letting me try this. I love you both."

I wiped my eyes and tried to settle down in the empty seat I had found in the middle of the darkened coach. The train was crowded and most of the passengers around me were asleep. I tried to get comfortable too, but it seemed impossible.

Rain began to slap at the window gently at first, then harder and harder. From time to time the sky trembled with white light. I closed my eyes and prayed. "I'm uneasy, God," I said, "but if you're with me, I'm ready for whatever comes." And then I added something I had been praying regularly. "I've been thinking that maybe there's a special reason for my taking this trip. You know that I've been asking for your help. Something's missing from my life—the special feeling that other Christians seem to have but I don't. Maybe you're just waiting for the right time to give it to me. I don't know, but I'll wait, too. Whatever you have in store for me, help me accept it."

The night deepened. The rain pounded harder on the windows. At last I drifted off to sleep until . . .

The sound of grinding metal. My seat shook. The car lurched. With a violent thrust I was thrown against the seat in front of me. I opened my eyes to see the seats around me buckling, luggage flying from overhead racks as the whole car leaned sideways.

Down I went on my knees, into the slanting aisle. . . .

Silence. And darkness. Then the cries of moans from stunned passengers.

"What happened?" a voice asked.

No one answered. No one knew the answer. I picked myself up slowly. I seemed to be OK. As my eyes adjusted to the darkness, I saw that the interior of our car was now tilted at a forty-five-degree angle. Suitcases were strewn everywhere. My watch said it was 3:20 A.M.

Somewhere in front of me, a woman started to scream, "We're in the water!"

Scrambling over scattered possessions, I looked out the window. The rain had stopped. There was a full moon, and in its eerie white light, I saw that we were surrounded by a torrent of rushing water.

"We're in the river," someone shouted. Suddenly there was hubbub.

"Careful!" someone else cried. "If we all move to the right, the car may tip over."

"We're all going to drown!" a woman screamed. "I know it. We're all going to drown!"

Confusion. Fright. Where were we? What should we do?

Then from somewhere not too far from me came a voice, this one strong and determined.

"Let's pray. *Let's pray.*"

Who can pray at a time like this? I thought. I was too panic-stricken about the water. I might be going off to be a camp counselor, but I still didn't know how to swim.

"C'mon," the voiced called again. "Doesn't anybody want to pray?"

My eyes met hers—even in the darkness, they were wide and bright against her black skin. She couldn't be much older than I was.

"What's your name?" she said. "Mine's Edna."

"I'm Sally," I answered shakily.

She grasped my hand and the hand of the boy in front of her, and told me to take the hand of an elderly woman nearby. "Our Father, who art in heaven," she began, speaking rapidly, "hallowed be thy name. . . ."

I still felt so dazed I couldn't keep up with her. Edna repeated the prayer again. As she spoke, my hands, clasped between the others', were feeling steadier.

"My Bible!" she said abruptly. "I need a light to read my Bible."

I remembered my dad's waterproof flashlight in my orange backpack. I groped around, found my backpack and the flashlight in it. I tried to use its light to get a good look at the damaged car—but Edna reached over and firmly directed its beam to her Bible. Even in the wavering glow, I could see the pages were worn and penciled with reference marks.

Edna read out loud. In the chaos of the car I could feel a calmness centering around Edna. And me.

"What about my luggage?" a lady kept asking.

"I've lost my shoes," another woman said. I felt around on the floor—and came up with a pair.

"No, those aren't mine," she said.

"But do you like them?" I said. As frightened as I had been, I was actually joking. When the lady laughed back, I felt her relief as well as mine.

The woman who had been screaming became even more hysterical. "We're all going to drown!" she cried again.

For an instant, my own fear surged once more.

I jumped as Edna grabbed my arm. "Listen to this!" She read in a loud voice the passage she had just come upon.

It was Psalm 69: "Save me, O God! For the waters have come up to my neck. I sink in deep mire, where there is no foothold; I have come into deep waters, and the flood sweeps over me."

I listened intently as she read on. "But as for me, my prayer is to thee, O Lord. At an acceptable time, O God, in the abundance of thy steadfast love answer me" (Psalm 69:1-2, 13, RSV).

In the window opposite, the light from my flashlight cast a reflection on the glass. I looked over and saw my own face—smiling! A smile that kept growing as the rest of me became relaxed and calm. Whatever happened, I knew we would be all right. I felt like laughing with joy. There was a "special feeling" growing inside me. God had answered my prayer at an "acceptable time" all right—in less than three hours!

"You believe, don't you, Sally?" Edna asked.

"I'm believing more and more all the time," I replied.

Edna prayed hard, telling God that two of his servants believed he was with us.

"I see lights!" somebody said. I saw them, too, in the distance—some of them glowing on boats making their way across the water toward us. Soon we heard the beat of helicopter blades overhead.

A conductor appeared at last. "I can't tell you for sure what's happened," he said. "We're just outside the little town of Emerson, Iowa, and I think we were hit by a flash flood. The tracks must have washed out and the train derailed." He told us that people in some of the other cars were actually in the water—and rescuers would help them out first. We should be safe in our car, he said, as long as we stayed put and didn't panic.

Another passenger and I helped the conductor pull out one of the emergency windows, and I was able to look out. The other cars in the train jutted in front and back of us at awkward angles—some of them had toppled almost completely over into the water.

I was calm as I talked and even joked with other passengers. Maybe because I had a flashlight people seemed to think I knew what was going on. One woman asked me if she could smoke.

"Ma'am," I said, amazed at my own politeness, "I can smell fuel. We don't need a fire now, too." She agreed—and actually looked reassured that someone knew what to do. Was this me talking?

As dawn neared, the water began to go down. We were in a field just next to a rain-swollen creek that had burst from its banks and washed out the railroad tracks—causing the train to derail and smash headlong into a bridge abutment. One young woman who had been between the cars of the train was killed. But of nearly three hundred others on the train, amazingly, most had only minor injuries.

In the morning, we were able to climb down out of the train and slosh our way along the tracks to a waiting school bus. We were transported to a local school, and there we learned that three nearby towns had been evacuated the night before because of flooding caused by the heavy rains.

The school had one pay phone, and everyone crowded around to call relatives. It was 7:05 A.M. when the operator put through a call to my home—and asked if anyone there would accept a collect call from Sally. Mom's voice shook as she answered. Only minutes before she and Dad had heard on the radio that the San Francisco Zephyr had derailed in a rapid river—and that there were many casualties. Mom and Dad had been crying and praying when my call came through.

I thought again of the note I had left them. "Whatever happens, please don't ever regret letting me try this."

Because now I know that whatever happens, I'm never alone. I've got a traveling companion who will never leave my side—God. He had never seemed closer. Or his presence so *special.*

"Mom, Mom," I called out over the telephone. "I'm all right."

Boy, was I ever.

THIRTY-ONE

Don't Ever Let Your Guard Down

BY DONALD JACKSON
EAGLE CREEK, OREGON

Don't ever think you're immune to trouble.

I was having a wonderful time. I was standing alone at the edge of Rosalyn Lake in sparsely settled country about twenty miles east of Portland, Oregon. Late-afternoon sunlight gilded the calm water. The air was chill—it was late November. Behind me Big Boy, my black Labrador retriever, fidgeted and whined. He was waiting for a pair of circling mallards to come within range. So was I.

I clicked off the safety catch on my twelve-gauge, double-barreled shotgun, feeling the excitement that every hunter knows. I was twenty-four years old, happily married. I had a good job in the construction business. I loved the outdoors. I was completely happy doing what I was doing. And I was about five seconds away from sudden death.

My decision to go hunting had been an impulsive one. A new stock had been put on my gun and I wanted to try it out. So I stuffed a few shells in my jeans, whistled to Big Boy, jumped into my car, and took off for the lake. I had never hunted it, but I figured some ducks might be there. I didn't tell my wife Brenda or anyone else where I was going (mistake number one). I figured I would be back in time for supper. Our friends Jeri and Eric Weber were coming over around eight.

Behind me Big Boy whined louder and plunged around, in and out of the water. Eagerness is a fine trait in a gun-dog, but a retriever has to learn to stay as still as a statue until he gets the order to retrieve. Ducks can spot any movement—and when they do, they are gone. I spoke urgently in a harsh whisper to Big Boy, but he didn't obey. I would have cuffed him with my hand, but he was just out of reach. I kept my eye on the ducks, sure they would be spooked by the dog. Big Boy kept moving until, exasperated, I did a very foolish thing. I shifted the gun to my right hand (mistake number two). Holding it by the barrels, I made an angry sweep behind me, hoping to freeze Big Boy into immobility.

What happened next was so sudden and shocking that I still can hardly believe it. Probably the screw in the new stock somehow came loose and allowed the trigger guard to depress the trigger. In any case, a stunning burst of sound shattered the quietness of the lake. Something like a gigantic fist slammed into my body just above my right hip. I was hurled into the water. Even as I fell, the unthinkable flashed across my mind in letters of fire. *I've shot myself!*

My first reaction was numbness and total shock. The water was not deep—ten inches perhaps. I tried to fire the three-shot SOS distress signal that hunters use in emergencies. But my slowness of reloading my two-shot gun made my signals ineffective. I tried to stand up, but my right leg felt paralyzed. I dragged myself out of the water. Again I tried to stand. Again I failed. I could not believe that this had happened to me, an experienced hunter, a firearms-safety fanatic.

A twelve-gauge shotgun is a deadly weapon of enormous power. A single shell loaded with Number Four shot—a heavy duck load—contains about 150 lead pellets. At forty or fifty yards they expand into a pattern eight or ten feet across, but at very close range they are condensed into an almost solid projectile that will tear a hole the size of a doorknob in almost anything. Such a hole was now blasted into my right side.

I tried to crawl away from the lake, but could manage only a few feet at a time. Then the pain began. Unbelievable pain. Later I learned that one pellet was carried by my bloodstream completely through the chambers of my heart and into one of my lungs. I was in such agony that I became nauseated. Then I couldn't breathe. At that point I said, "Lord, if you're going to take me home, please do it quickly. Or else help me with this pain." The moment I said that, the pain lessened. I knew then that I had a chance of surviving because the Lord was right there, listening to me.

All my life I have felt close to the Lord. My parents are missionaries far up in the northern part of Canada. They believe in miracles, and they taught us children to believe in them too. I didn't know it then, but one extraordinary miracle had already taken place: Incredibly, the charge of shot had not gone all the way through my body. It had stopped inside, tearing away muscles, nicking one kidney, damaging the liver—but missing the spine. If one pellet had gone all the way through, I would have bled to death.

Somehow I kept crawling until I came to a tree. Big Boy stayed with me, puzzled and troubled. Anxious now to please, he brought a stick for me to throw. This frightened me because he could be very rough and insistent whenever we played fetch. "Lord," I murmured, "I can't handle this." And for the first time in his life, Big Boy broke off the game before it had even started and lay down quietly beside me.

I lay huddled under the tree, watching the light fade out of the sky. A pale moon began to glow above the lake. The temperature was dropping. My wet clothing offered little protection. Soon, I knew people would be looking for me. I wondered if the moonlight would help them. I wondered how they would know where to look. I thought of Brenda, and how much I loved her. I figured I could hang on until morning. With the Lord's help—and maybe Big Boy's warmth.

Meantime, back at our house, Brenda was puzzled when I didn't appear for supper. By the time the Webers arrived, she was starting to worry. She telephoned her father, John Van Diest, who is publisher of the Multnomah Press in Portland. A close friend and working companion in the construction business, Blair Andersen, arrived. By ten o'clock they were all out looking. They checked places where they knew I sometimes hunted. Nothing. A fog began rolling in, blotting out the moonlight. Everyone was doing a lot of praying.

Despite her tears, Brenda remained very steady, very calm. When you ask the Lord to supply your needs, he does. About midnight Brenda's father called from the area where he was searching and suggested she search the Rosalyn Lake area, although he warned it was an unlikely place for me to hunt. She took off in one of the cars with Jeri and Eric, but now the fog was so dense that they lost a lot of time because visibility was down to about fifteen feet. It was about 2:15 A.M. when they found themselves creeping along one of the roads near the lake. Suddenly Eric braked to a stop. "Thought I saw something glimmer," he said. Sure enough, it was a car. Everything intact.

Eric shouted my name at the top of his lungs. Then he listened. "There!" he said to the girls. "Did you hear that?" They had heard nothing. Again he shouted. Again the girls heard nothing, but Eric's sharp ears caught a faint, far-off sound. It was my feeble voice, trying to answer him. Incredibly, I was still conscious.

By now the temperature was down to thirty-three degrees. My voice was weak from thirst and loss of blood. I had tried to suck water from my soaked parka all night, but my throat was almost too dry for me to speak. So I tried to whistle. A few moments later Eric came plunging through the woods and found me.

They couldn't move me. I'm six foot three and heavy. They had to find a farmhouse, wake up the people, and ask them to call the volunteer fire department in the little town of Sandy. Those guys were magnificent. In a little while there were about six vehicles, including police and ambulance, standing by with all sorts of emergency equipment. They tried to give me an IV, but I had lost so much blood they couldn't find a vein. My body temperature was down to ninety-four degrees. Doctors said later that in one more hour I would have been dead from exposure.

My rescuers carried me out of the woods. Then they radioed for a rescue helicopter. Amazingly, the pilot found a hole in the fog and landed near us there in Sandy. They flew to Gresham Hospital where, again amazingly, the fog thinned enough for them to land. The minute they landed, it closed in again. They were stuck there for several hours.

A medical team was waiting. By 7:00 A.M. I was in surgery. The doctors worked for almost three hours, repairing torn tissues. They removed dozens of lead pellets, but they had to leave a lot of them in. Then the surgeon came out and told Brenda and her parents that I had made it through the operation. For the first time, Brenda broke down and cried.

The doctors were afraid of gangrene. All the conditions for it were present. But thanks to their skill and the Lord's protection, it never developed. I was in three different hospitals for a total of a month, but now, two years later, I'm about as good as ever.

I almost lost my life that afternoon, but I gained two things that are going to stay with me for the rest of my days. The first—and this is a message for outdoorsmen and hunters everywhere—is this: Don't *ever* think you're immune to trouble. Don't *ever* let your guard down. Don't *ever* forget the dangers involved in what you're doing. In a way, the more experienced you are, the more risk there may be, because you get overconfident and then you get careless—as I did—for just a split second. That split second can cost you your life or the life of another hunter. No matter how confident you are, you can never be sure.

Likewise—and I think this is the most important thing I have to pass on—you can never be sure about how much time you have left in this life. Standing there on the shore of Rosalyn Lake, I was just twenty-four years old—strong, healthy, confident, brimming with life and vitality. The next instant I was staring straight into the blank eyes of death.

If you think there is time left in the future to get your spiritual life in order, then think again. The time to make a decision about that is now. What if you never have another chance?

This whole experience has left me changed in other ways. At least Brenda says it has. She says I'm no longer so ambitious in a material sense. I used to plan on moving up fast in the construction business. Not anymore. Now I'm back in Bible school, trying to improve my education, trying to figure out how I can be of service to people.

I don't worry about what the exact field of service may be. When the time comes, I'll ask the Lord to tell me.

I know he will.

THIRTY-TWO

Lifelines

BY CATHY BALDRIDGE
MILLSTADT, ILLINOIS

A string of strange events—and then the accident.

It was a strange few days.

As I listen to the tornado watch on the radio that Friday afternoon, I go to the kitchen window. The sky beyond the town water tower does look dark and, to be safe, I decide to take my two little ones—Dawn, three, and Jeremy, a year—and the two young girls I'm baby-sitting down to the basement. I should be used to this—in our part of Illinois, in the summer, we have tornado watches all the time—but I can't help being fearful.

And as we settle into a corner of the cellar, I can see the children are scared. Especially the girls I'm baby-sitting—Lisa and Kim. They are older and know what tornados can do. So I tell them a story.

In simple terms, I tell them about when my parents, in World War II, were prisoners in a German labor camp somewhere near Bonn. It was a horrible place—cold, little to eat—and the last few months of the war were the worst as the Allied bombs fell every day. The Allies, of course, didn't mean to bomb prisoners, but that didn't make the bombs any less deadly.

Most of the prisoners were very frightened, and at first so were my mom and dad. They had no safe place to hide. The Germans kept the best bomb shelters for themselves.

But instead of giving in to fear, my parents and a few others began to pray and sing hymns. Others shouted, "What are you doing? Are you crazy?" But my mom and dad knew God was their only hope and refuge. They fought off the awful scream of bombs with their prayers, and ultimately God brought them through.

I stop my storytelling. Outside a heavy rain has begun to fall. We'll be all right.

"And so you see," I say to the children, "we don't have to be too afraid of a tornado. God will answer if we ask him to keep us safe."

We say a prayer, but the children are still unsettled, and it is not until we are upstairs again, where we can see the sky clearing, that their fears are eased.

The children go back to playing and I begin to prepare dinner. We eat early because I give piano lessons in the early evening. My thoughts go back to the story of my parents. It always stirs the same feelings in me—excitement, but also confusion, even despair.

It always makes me wonder. Why haven't I ever felt God's presence the way Mom and Dad did? My father, who died eight years ago, was so faith-filled. And my mother's faith still makes her so strong. So much more than I am. But after what Mom and Dad went through, how can I expect my faith to be as deep?

I can't, I say to myself.

True, my husband Ray and I have had our troubles. When Dawn was one year old, she nearly died of pneumonia. And Jeremy had ear problems. And then, too, Ray's deafness in one ear has made work hard to find. Just recently he was unemployed for ten months.

But these troubles had been only dreary burdens. They didn't show God's presence in the way my parents' ordeal had. Not for me, at least.

Ray comes home from work and reads the paper at the kitchen table while I cook. During dinner, Dawn and Jeremy make most of the noise. I try to keep the kids reined in so that they won't get on Ray's nerves.

My piano lesson after dinner does not go very well. The pupil is struggling with the chords, and I'm not much help to her. I know I should be more energetic, but this dull weight seems to have settled over me. At the end of the lesson my pupil leaves forlornly, and I tell myself, *You'd better get with it, Cathy, or that girl will lose interest in the piano for good.*

The weekend passes quickly. I have plans for the time but don't carry them out. I want to spend some special time with Ray, but I let little things get in the way. In church on Sunday my mind wanders.

Monday comes, bringing a new week of chores, and I've no energy to take them on. As I go about my tasks, I know that I should take time to read Scripture. Maybe God's strong words would chase away this weak feeling. But I give in to the routine of the day. It's easy to do.

Late in the afternoon I sit back and watch television. Here is a time when I could give a few moments to God. But, no, to do errands today I had to borrow my mother's car and soon I'll have to pick her up at work.

At about 5:15, Ray comes through the door. He doesn't look right. He looks shaken up, and I ask him what's wrong.

"On the way home," he says, sitting down, "just outside St. Louis, I came on an accident that had happened a moment before. A car with a couple and a child in it crashed into the guardrail. I helped get them settled until the ambulance came. The father looked pretty badly hurt, but I think he'll be OK. Still, it scares you. . . ."

As Ray's voice trails off, I tell him he was good to have stopped.

"It's really the least I could do."

"You were still good." I then tell Ray that I wish I could stay and sit with him, but I've got to pick up Mom.

As Dawn and Jeremy and I go, Ray says, "Please be careful, Cathy. Extra careful."

Going out the door I say I will. Before I pick up my mother, I have to drop Dawn off at baton lessons. Then Jeremy and I are alone, driving along in the old Maverick. Jeremy, strapped into his car seat, is soon asleep. Traffic isn't too heavy. It looks as if I'll reach my mother's shop in time.

But as I approach the railroad crossing in Swansea, the red lights suddenly begin flashing and, before I can slip through, the barrier gate swings down.

I come to a stop in one of the outside lanes of the four-lane road. It is 5:45. I hope the coming train won't be a long, long freight.

A horn honks behind me. In the rearview mirror I see a car—a big old Plymouth Fury—coming up fast behind me. The woman driving it honks again. I mutter to myself, "Where do you want me to go, lady?"

When I see that she is going to pass by me in the inside lane—and, I guess, sneak around the gate—I'm glad. I glance down at Jeremy to see if he has been disturbed. He is still sleeping soundly.

This innocent sight suddenly bursts into pieces. As if we have been hit by a bomb, our car explodes with a horrible crashing and grinding of metal. We spin and slide and I feel as if my head is being torn from my shoulders. Then there is another violent smash as we careen into the wooden crossing gate.

Jeremy is screaming, but as I reach down for him, the woman in the Fury hits us once more, broadside, and when I look up and see her, I think, *She must be trying to kill us. She's driven us right onto the tracks!*

And Jeremy. By his screams I'm sure he has broken his neck. I carefully feel his neck and back with my hands. He seems to be in one piece.

The next thing I hear freezes me with fright. A train whistle blows, and though the train is still out of sight, I know it is not far off—just around that near bend.

I try to open my door, but it is smashed in and, worse, the Fury is pinned up against it. I yell to the driver to back up.

She tries to start her car, but the fan grinds against the pushed-in radiator. The car won't start. In shock, helpless, the woman gets out of her car and walks away.

Crazy with fear, I look all around our car for an escape. The passenger-side door. I reach across Jeremy and try it. No. That side of the car is pinned against the gatepost.

The whistle blows again, now more like a heavy shriek. "Why won't anybody help us?" I scream.

Panicked, I think that Jeremy and I should huddle in the backseat. I'll shield my baby. In the back of my mind I know the idea is foolish, but I can't think further.

Then a voice outside cries, "Get out! Get out! You've got to get out!"

"We can't," I scream. "We're trapped!"

I hear boards crackling, and then see a brown-haired woman—about my age and very small—wading through the debris of the broken gate. Again she says, "Get out. Look! You've got to!"

Then I see it. Headlight shining, whistle blowing, the huge dark locomotive comes around the bend. It is no more than a few hundred yards away. I want with all my might to hear the brakes start screeching.

The woman grabs the passenger-side door. The stub of the gate holds the door clamped shut. With all she has got, the woman pulls at the door. It opens five or six inches.

"That's the best I can do," she says. "You'll have to squeeze."

I crouch on the hump between the bucket seats and try to unstrap Jeremy from his car seat. My fingers feel like lifeless twigs.

"Please, Lord," I pray, "don't let me lose my mind now."

Finally I get Jeremy loose, and then, crawling to the door, I try to squeeze us through the narrow slot. It is useless. We won't fit.

So I plead to the woman, "Please take my baby," and simultaneously, she says, "Give him to me!"

I press Jeremy into the opening and the woman grabs his arm and pulls him through. As she carries Jeremy to safety, I hear his cries trail away. *At least he'll survive.*

The train is now not even fifty feet away. I'm alone. The locomotive looks like a monster in a nightmare, unbelievable, huge, and murderous. It is roaring. Why hasn't the engineer braked? I writhe and twist, trying to wedge myself through. Now a man is at the side of the tracks, trying to flag the train down. I look over at the woman who holds my baby. She is yelling, but I can't hear her. "Lord, let me live if only for the sake of Jeremy. And Ray. And Dawn."

Closing my eyes, twisting. I try one more time to slink through.

And suddenly I'm free. It stuns me. But the horrible roar tells me to run, and just as I get away, I look back and see my car crumple under the iron wheels of the train.

This sight sends me into a numb daze. And I don't really begin to come out of it until I have been taken to a Dairy Queen across the street, where people sit me down. There, with Jeremy in my arms, I realize I haven't thanked the woman who rescued us. Where is she? No one knows. Not until the next day will I learn her name. Joyce Johnson.

Jeremy and I are taken to a hospital where, amazingly, we are found to be uninjured. In what seems a strangely short time, the two of us are home with Ray and Dawn.

We came so close to death! As I tell Ray the story of the accident, that fact begins to terrify me all over again, but then I remember the woman who rescued us and, as I picture her courage, all I can feel is awe.

When I tell Ray about her, he says, "We should thank God for putting good people like that woman in bad places."

Thank God. I do have to thank God for Joyce Johnson. As I sit in a rocking chair, safe in our living room, I can see that God came to my rescue. Just as he came to the rescue of my parents. In this case, God had come to me through Joyce. She had opened the door with God's help. She had taken my child to safety, enabling me to free myself.

And, in this sudden awakening light, I now can see that God has often come to my rescue, just as Ray says, *by putting good people in bad places.* There were the nurses who had perked up my spirits when my children were sick. And there were the friends who helped us out during Ray's unemployment. And then, just this very afternoon, my own husband had come to the aid of those three people in the car accident.

It's clear. When you are in pain, the care of good people drives off the fear of being forsaken. They are God's lifelines. And through them, finally, I feel the presence of God.

THIRTY-THREE

The Precious Hours

BY LAURA NORMAN
MISSOULA, MONTANA

The locker door was frozen shut.
I was trapped.

Strange, the thoughts that come to mind when you think you are dying. How odd that all those matters that were so important at 8:00 A.M., 10:00 A.M., even noon, fade into fog as your life begins to slip away at 2:00. Obviously I speak from experience—the experience of only a day ago.

Eight A.M. The Montana "ranch" I live on is no longer a working operation, but it is still my home. I have worked and lived on this place since the day I came here as a bride. Winters have been hard, the work never done, but always there has been new life and growing things.

Years ago, in the north bedroom of this house, I gave birth to a tiny baby girl. It was not planned that way—but she was born in January, the year of the big blizzard, and there was no way to travel the hundred miles to a hospital. My husband helped, and the wife of one of the hired hands, and it was all worthwhile once I held her in my arms.

After my husband passed away, it is no wonder that I decided to live on here. Cows continue to calve in the spring, and only yesterday a little colt wobbled to its feet outside my window. But it is different now. The animals are no longer my concern. The land around the house has been sold.

Maybe this is why the lilac bushes I planted myself mean so much to me, why I take such care to coax the tulips to bloom along the path and watch each blossom come to life on the apple tree.

I am busy. I keep the house spotless and do the painting and repairs I never had time to do before. I am content. I take an active part in church affairs. And, above all, I give little thought to dying. If someone should ask me, I would say, "God is in his heaven, and I am here. Meeting him on a personal basis is an event that will happen sometime in the future."

Ten A.M. A call from my daughter Margaret (now all grown up with a child of her own). She says they will be driving over from the city after Michael's nap. Michael, my grandson, is almost three and one of the greatest joys of my life. I love watching him meet each new experience with wonder. Even the grass turning warm and green is a pleasure to his little feet.

"I'd better put him down soon for a little shuteye," my daughter tells me on the phone, "or he will be a grizzly bear."

After I hang up, I feel a thrill of anticipation—and so much to do! I must dust the house and do a bit of laundry and thaw some meat for supper. If time permits, I might finish the tiny pair of pull-on jeans I'm sewing for Michael.

Jim, my daughter's husband, will be coming too, and that in itself is a treat. As a struggling young attorney, his weekends are often spoken for. But he is taking this Saturday off, and they will all three be here. Swiss steak—they like that—cooked with my home-canned tomatoes and pared onions. Yes, today will be very busy—very busy indeed!

I hum a little tune as I dust and straighten the house. Then I head for the basement, my arms full of laundry. As I start down the stairs I suddenly think of Michael, and a day last winter when he was visiting me. It was getting dark outside, and Michael was kneeling beside his bed saying his prayers.

"God bless Daddy," he said, "and God bless Mommy," and then there was a pause.

"And God bless Grandma," I prodded gently.

He turned his face to look up at me with his large, brown eyes. "But, Grandma," he said. "God already blesses you."

Going down the stairs, watching the steps around the load of laundry I carry, I think how very true his statement is.

Down here in the basement the air seems close, so I open the door into the yard. Sunlight makes a bright pattern on the floor, and the breeze brings indoors the spring smells of new grass, wild flower, and dandelions. I can hear a bird singing his heart out in an apple tree.

I can remember when washers were not automatic, but this machine is, so after loading and pushing all necessary buttons, I go down the hall to the locker to get the Swiss steak out to thaw.

It is a large walk-in locker, perhaps six feet by four, large enough to hold several quarters of beef extended on hooks from the low ceiling. No need now for all that meat, but I still keep frozen packages on the shelves that line the locker.

As I bend to select a package, I hear the large, heavy door close gently behind me. I feel a start of surprise that the wind from the yard is strong enough to close it, but no matter! My husband installed this locker himself, years ago, and on the inside he carefully placed a large metal knob that, when pushed, will open the locker door.

The knob looks frosted, so I wrap my apron around it before pushing. It does not budge. I place my package of wrapped meat on the floor, and using my apron, I try with both hands. No response! I wrap both my hands around the plunger that extends from the knob. I leave them there until the slight accumulated frost has melted. When I pull my hands away I feel acute pain from the coldness, but I try again, pushing the weight of my body against the knob. It will not even move!

Well now, I tell myself, *do not panic. Find something to knock it loose. The plunger has simply frozen a bit in the shaft.*

I take off my apron and tie it around my neck, making a shawl to cover my bare arms. Shivering, I look around. Nothing. No hooks, no hammer, nothing—except packages of frozen meat. All right then, one of those will have to do.

I select a package that protrudes enough at one end to form a sort of handle. By now my hands are becoming numb, and I drop it twice before getting a firm hold. *Now, do it right the first time,* I tell myself. *You have to hit it hard enough to break the frost loose.*

I set my feet apart, hold the frozen package firmly, and bring it down on the round metal knob with a thud. I hear it crack. *Good,* I think, *now push.* I grab the knob in both hands to push, and the knob comes loose in my grasp! For almost a minute I stand there staring at the plunger, broken loose from the knob with no way to send it through the shaft to open the door.

I sit down hard on an old packing box and stare at the door, hugging my apron around me. The air seems hard to breathe. I wonder how long it takes a person to freeze in this temperature. *What nonsense, I must keep trying, keep thinking. Let's see, Margaret and Jim are coming, but after Michael's nap. An hour? Three hours, most likely. Too late!*

My neighbor who does the yard work for me sometimes comes on Saturday. Can I make myself be heard? I try to scream his name as loud as I can, but even to me the sound seems muted. Then I remember. Today he has taken the lawn mower to town to get it sharpened. Probably will not bring it back until evening. Again, too late!

Why didn't I place something against the door? I ask myself. *Why did I open the basement door so that the wind could blow in? Why was I so foolish?*

Foolish or not, I have always been a very practical person. Sitting here on a box, my legs now drawn up under me, my apron tucked around my knees, I face the likely possibility . . . of death.

I have heard it said that in the last hour or minutes before death a person's whole life passes before him. It is not happening to me. Instead, I keep remembering instances, a circumstance here, a word there. Suddenly it seems almost real.

The night my daughter was born I kept praying, "Dear God, bring the baby through this. Keep it healthy. Do not let anything happen to the baby." Had I remembered to thank God?

And my daughter, Margaret, six years old. "Mom, look what I made for you."

"Not now, dear," I had answered. "Can't you see mother is busy?"

And my husband standing in the doorway, twisting his hat in his hands. "I was thinking," he said, "maybe we could take some time off, go to one of those church retreats, be alone together . . . away from things?"

"I cannot be gone that long," I replied.

Why had I been so busy?

Oh, yes. God remembered me, over and over again, but was I too busy to love and care? Was I too busy to remember him? Why has

God never seemed a personal friend? Is it because I didn't have the time to seek his friendship?

No, I tell myself, in all honesty. I am not an evil person, but neither am I very good. Average perhaps.

And now, when I need his help so desperately, when I am helpless on my own, would "average" be good enough? How can I ask him for anything? I don't really know him.

I close my eyes and the lids seem to be sticking, too heavy to open. Yet it seems I can see my daughter sitting across from me at the kitchen table. I recall I was peeling potatoes, and Michael was running back and forth, bringing me one spoon at time from the drawer.

"I really should not have been so hard on her," I was saying about some person, "but she let things drag along, so I told her what I thought of her" . . . but now, I am sorry. I do not know why I said such a thing.

One foot keeps slipping out from under me . . . my leg has no feeling . . . *Who was "she"?* I wonder. *To whom had I been so unkind?* I cannot remember.

Then my daughter was talking. "Now, Mother," she said, "why berate yourself? If you have asked God for forgiveness, I am sure he has forgiven you. If God has forgiven you, Mother, why can't you forgive yourself?"

Suddenly, I know that is the answer! I see those words written across my sluggish consciousness in flaming light. *So often God forgives,* I think, *but we cannot forgive ourselves. The channel between us and him remains clogged with feelings of guilt.*

My head falls upon my chest. Now, at last, I can pray.

"O Father," I murmur, "I forgive myself, even as you have forgiven me. I plead for your mercy, Lord, and I place myself in your hands. The darkness is closing around me now, but I can see the light of your love at the other end of the dark tunnel. I come to you just as I am—good and bad together—trusting in your love. Now I can see that the door of your love is opening, a warm breeze reaches me, taking with it the numbing cold. . . ."

I can feel a warm blanket being wrapped around me, and voices—where are the voices coming from? Someone is carrying me out of the locker, out into the warm hall . . . and there is light coming through a door, and then there is warm, wonderful darkness.

Later, much later, my daughter is standing by the hospital bed, and she is saying, ". . . and Michael was so excited about going to see

Grandma, he would not take his nap, so we came much earlier than we had planned."

Jim is there also, standing beside my pillow; ". . . a combination of circumstances," he is saying. "Steam from the laundry room froze in the mechanism."

And I am thinking, *Thank you, God, for teaching me to make you the center of my life, for teaching me that even your gift of forgiveness requires forgiveness from me. Thank you, O Lord, for all the joys of my life, and for the adversities that make the joys more acute. Thank you for answering my prayers, for being near me, for caring, and above all, O Father, thank you for this personal walk with you.*

THIRTY-FOUR

What on Earth Is Shoo-fly Pie Anyway?

BY MARY HELEN LIVINGSTON
COLUMBIA, SOUTH CAROLINA

AMISH SHOO-FLY PIE
(Yield two 8-inch pies)

Crumb Mixture
2 cups flour
¾ cup brown sugar
⅓ cup lard, shortening, or butter
½ teaspoon nutmeg (optional)
1 teaspoon cinnamon (optional)

Thoroughly mix above ingredients together in a bowl until crumbs are formed. Line two 8-inch pie plates with half the crumb mixture, reserving the remaining half for topping.

Syrup Mixture
1 cup molasses
½ cup brown sugar
2 eggs
1 cup hot water
1 teaspoon baking soda dissolved in hot water

In a separate bowl, mix syrup ingredients thoroughly. Pour half of the syrup mixture into each unbaked crumb-lined pie plate, then sprinkle remaining crumb mixture on top. Bake at 400° F for 10 minutes, then reduce heat to 350° F and continue baking for 50 minutes more. Cool before eating.

The doctor closed his bag and turned to me. "Call me if he gets any worse this afternoon or tonight. I'll stop by in the morning to see him. If he's no better, I'll have to put him in the hospital. He needs fluids, and he must eat."

"I've given him everything I can think of, but he just can't keep anything down."

"You must keep on trying. He is getting weak and dehydrated. Do your best. I'll see you tomorrow morning."

I sat down in the rocking chair by the sofa where my little son lay. Bobby had always been thin and undersized. Now, after days of battling an especially severe form of influenza, he looked wan and wasted. What would I do if he had to be hospitalized? I was a nursing student at Florida State University in Tallahassee and had no hospitalization insurance and very little money. What if the hospital refused to admit him?

I prayed silently, "Lord, show me what to do."

"Bobby, suppose I go to the store and buy a different kind of soup for you. And maybe some Jell-O. Don't you think you might be able to eat some?"

"No, Mama."

"Can't you think of anything you'd like?"

"Make me some shoo-fly pie, Mama. I could eat that. I know I could."

Bobby had never eaten shoo-fly pie in his life. He could not desire something he had never seen or tasted. Yet I knew why he had asked. To pass the long, weary hours of illness, I had been reading stories to him from library books. *Yonie Wondernose* by Marguerite De Angeli was his favorite. It was the story of Johnny, a little Amish boy from the Pennsylvania Dutch area, and it described vividly the customs, dress, food, and daily activities of the Amish.

My life had been spent in Georgia and Florida. I knew nothing of the Amish, had never seen an Amish person, had never tasted a Pennsylvania Dutch dish. What on earth is shoo-fly pie? A custard pie? A savory meat concoction like shepherd's pie? The little story had mentioned shoo-fly pie, but had failed to list the ingredients. I doubted the wisdom of experimenting with strange, exotic foods in the middle of a serious illness. However, it was the only food Bobby had requested and maybe it was worth trying. Whatever was in it, it was probably not going to stay in him long enough to do any harm.

Having made the decision to act on Bobby's request, I set about locating a recipe. The Leon County Library did not have a book on Pennsylvania Dutch cookery and neither did the State Library. The library at Florida State University had such a cookbook, but it was in use and not due back for two weeks. I called nearby bookstores. They had no Pennsylvania Dutch cookbooks. I called my neighbors, friends, relatives. Some of them had heard of shoo-fly pie, but none of them knew what it was.

"Bobby, there isn't a recipe for shoo-fly pie in this town. I'm just as sorry as I can be. After you are well, we will try again, but right now we are going to have to do with what we can get. I'm going to the grocery store now and try to find something easy for you to eat. Your grandfather will sit with you while I'm gone."

"What store are you going to, Mama? I'll ask God to send you a recipe there. He'll send you one."

"Oh, no, Bobby," I said in alarm, "please don't do that!" I couldn't bear the thought of his faith being shattered. And there was obviously no way for God to provide a recipe in a grocery store. I had already tried all the likely places. It would be best for Bobby not to ask for the impossible.

"God will know how to send you a recipe, Mama. Are you going to Winn-Dixie?"

"Yes, I'm going to Winn-Dixie. Don't ask God, honey. I'll be back soon with something good."

In Winn-Dixie I pushed my shopping cart, filling it with red and green Jell-O, butterscotch pudding, chicken noodle soup. And then, nearing the checkout counter, I stood still, not believing what I saw. Walking in the door were two women, one wearing a black prayer cap, the other a white one, just like the pictures in *Yonie Wondernose*. Hurrying toward them, I asked, "Are you Amish?"

"Yes, we are Amish."

"And do you know how to make shoo-fly pie?"

"Of course. All Amish women know how to make shoo-fly pie."

"Could you write me a recipe?"

"Why, yes, certainly. If you have paper, I'll write it down, and then we will help you find the things you need to make a nice pie."

As we walked around gathering brown sugar, molasses, and spices, I asked them if they lived in Tallahassee.

"Oh, goodness, no! We are just passing through. We have been down in Florida and are on our way back home to Pennsylvania. I don't know why we stopped in here, but all of a sudden, my companion said, 'Let's stop at that Winn-Dixie.' So here we are. I really don't know why we came in."

Awestruck, humbled, and ashamed, I knew why. Bobby had disobeyed me. He had asked—and received.

When I walked into the living room with the groceries, Bobby said, "You got the recipe God sent, didn't you, Mama?"

The recipe made not one, but two large shoo-fly pies. Bobby ate almost the whole pie during the late afternoon and early evening and drank several cups of weak tea. Moreover, he retained all he ate and drank. The pie, high in carbohydrates, provided energy, and the tea replaced lost body fluids. By morning, Bobby was able to drink fruit juices and eat poached eggs and toast. His improvement thereafter was rapid and dramatic.

And so, after all these years there's a letter I want to write:

Dear Amish Ladies;

This story is really a long-overdue letter to you. It should have been written immediately after this incident, which happened so many years ago. I thought it was in 1954; Bobby says it was 1955. His grandfather would remember exactly, but he died in 1976 and I cannot ask him. Please forgive me for not getting your names and addresses. How could I have been so preoccupied with my problems that I failed to provide myself with the means of thanking you two for the parts you played in this drama?

Perhaps, not knowing the beginning or end of the story, you regarded it as a trivial incident and pushed it away into the vast storehouse of forgetfulness. I want to jog your memory. You had been on a pleasure trip to Florida with friends and were driving back home. You passed through the business district of Tallahassee, Florida. You were driving north on Monroe Street, the highway to Thomasville, Georgia, when you came to a Winn-Dixie on your right. Do you remember?

I want you to remember, because for me this was not a happenstance, a coincidence. Through the years, when my faith has faltered, when cynicism has threatened me, I find myself thinking of a very sick child making a simple request that he knew *would be granted. Unlike me, Bobby wasn't concerned with* how *God was going to go about it; he trusted in his infinite power. It reminds me that I have no right to wish my own human limitations on God, for with God all things are possible. Thank you, dear Amish ladies, for being his messengers.*

THIRTY-FIVE

The Premonition

BY J. V. CALVERT
FORT WORTH, TEXAS

I was a tough, no-nonsense truck driver. What were these strange feelings that kept nagging at me?

"What is it, Lord? What's this weird feeling that something unpleasant is waiting for me down the road?"

As usual, I was talking to my Friend as I drove through the muggy August night at 3:00 A.M., hauling 48,000 pounds of steel in my eighteen-wheel rig.

I knew nothing mechanical was wrong. As careful truckers do, I had done a thorough job of checking everything before leaving on this round-trip run between Forth Worth and Bryan, Texas. The only thing I had found to worry me was a creepy spider skittering across the dashboard. I'm six feet two and fifty-two years old, but I'm a baby about spiders. Using my leather driving gloves, I'd brushed it out of the cab.

But now this strange sixth sense was telling me that I ought to be extra careful, extra wide-awake. I had never had it before, and I kept trying to turn it over to the Lord.

"Lord God. You're my Father, and I know you want what's best for all your children. So now I ask you to ride this run with me—sit really close; keep me alert; help me get rid of this crazy feeling that's bugging me. I give you the honor and the glory."

A lot of truckers are big on CB-radio talk for passing the time. I would rather talk to the Lord. I had grown up in a family where talking to him and singing his praises were as natural as breathing. So on the long, dark, lonesome runs I make for Central Freight Lines, it is second nature for me to ask him to keep me company. Each night I always pray and sing the old familiar hymns. Doing that helps me feel ready for any surprises that might come my way. But this night I couldn't seem to relax.

By 6:45 A.M. I had picked up my return load of 43,000 pounds of bleach and was on my way back to Fort Worth. I planned to make my usual breakfast stop at the Dixie Cafe. But when I got there and parked—do you know that sneaky uneasiness wouldn't let me go in? *Don't stop now,* came the urging. *Keep on moving down the road.*

I sat still a few seconds, trying to resist it, thinking about juice and eggs and coffee. Then my hand reached for the ignition switch.

With something like a groan, I began to ease the rig out of the parking lot. *J. V.,* I told myself, *you can handle a truck just fine, but this fool thing going on in your head is something else.* And then I prayed, "Please, Lord, I'm counting on you to stay here in this cab with me."

Out on Highway 6, I concentrated on the road. Only two lanes wide, it didn't give a tractor trailer much room for maneuvering. Unconsciously, I began to sing again; "Jesus loves me, this I know, for the Bible tells me so. . . ." I hadn't sung *that* since I was a little kid.

About thirty miles from Waco, I glanced in my side-view mirror and saw a trucker coming up fast on my tail. He was in an empty truck or he wouldn't have been able to highball it like that. Since I was hauling a slow, heavy load, I pulled over to let the empty truck overtake me. As the driver whizzed by, he raised his hand in the traditional signal that says, "Thanks, good buddy." Soon he was three hundred yards down the highway.

And then it happened. Sitting high in my cab, thirteen feet off the ground, I had a bird's-eye view of the trucker's nightmare unfolding in front of me. In a flash, something happened and his big rig went out of control. It reeled across the wrong side of Highway 6 and careened along the shoulder. Then, on a slight incline some seventy-five yards off the highway, it flipped over, jackknifed and turned bottom-side up. I heard a monstrous *vroom,* as if a giant match had been struck. Fire and black smoke mushroomed from the cab area.

I had already stopped my rig a safe distance away. Now I raced down the highway, my knees pumping like pistons. "Oh, Lord, have mercy," I prayed as I charged toward the fiery cab.

When I came around the truck and saw the driver, I thought he was a goner. His bleeding head and shoulders were wedged in the broken window behind the steel supporting braces of the big side mirror. The braces were bent so they formed prison bars, and the bottom of the mirror was embedded deep in the ground.

"Oh, Lord, have mercy! Give me the power to yank that stuff loose!"

Just then, the man moaned and I knew he was alive. I took a deep breath, grabbed the mess of steel braces and half-buried mirror, and jerked it with all my strength. Unbelievably, the whole thing broke free!

Please, God, don't let him be stuck in that flaming cab.

"You're gonna have to try and help me, buddy," I pleaded. The trucker's arms were pinned to his sides, but he began to move.

"That's it! Keep wiggling!" I pulled and eased him out of the cab window frame onto the ground.

Oh, God, let us get away from this truck before its gas tanks explode.

I helped the man up, and he began stumbling up the incline on his own. But he was in shock—covered with blood, dirt, and shattered glass—and he collapsed on the grass almost immediately. We had to get farther away.

It was then I looked up, acutely aware that something very unusual was going on. The wind was out of the south, more than just a breeze. Fire and smoke should have been billowing in our direction. In fact, the wind should have blown fire and smoke directly on me as I was dragging the driver out of his burning cab. But it hadn't. Instead, I could see the smoke swirling straight up, arching over the truck—over us—and coming down in the middle of the highway like a rainbow. How long could it last?

Frantically, I helped the man get up again. Just as we reached a safe distance about fifty yards away, the gas tanks blew, incinerating the tractor trailer as if it were just a wad of dry paper. And at that instant, the smoke and fire began blowing the way they should have all along—igniting the area we had left only seconds before.

"Thank you, Almighty Lord!"

Suddenly people began appearing out of nowhere, beating out the grass fire, and then gathering around us—another truck driver, motorists who had stopped. In the distance, I could hear an ambulance siren.

Someone showed up with a first-aid kit. Other people started picking glass out of the man's shirt and cleaning him up. The ambulance arrived. So did the highway patrol and a local fire department. My job was done.

As I was walking toward my truck, a bystander caught up with me. "Hey, you saved that man's life! No one else had the guts to go near that truck—scared it would blow any second."

I shook my head. "I don't want the credit," I told him. "I just try to stay close in touch with the Lord. So when I need help, he's there to give it. He gave me the push and the strength and a couple of miracles this morning, and he gets the glory."

I thought for a minute and then I started to chuckle. "You think I've got guts? Why, man, you're looking at a guy who's scared of a little spider!"

THIRTY-SIX

It's So Cold and Hope Is So Hard to Find

BY STEVE SMART
PORT MANSFIELD, TEXAS

On Christmas Eve, 1981, a small, six-seat Cherokee plane carrying five people crashed onto a remote ridge high on one of the most rugged ranges of Colorado's Rocky Mountains. Gary Meeks, a Dallas construction executive, was piloting the plane that carried his wife, Pat, his two sons—Arnie, eighteen, and Darren, fifteen—and a family friend and former business associate, Steve Smart, thirty-four. They were on their way to a skiing vacation in Aspen when the plane seemed to lose power. All survived the subsequent crash landing, but, with Pat seriously hurt and Steve unconscious, Gary left the plane to search for help. More than twenty-four hours later Steve slowly regained consciousness. Here is Steve's story of what followed.

Friday, Christmas Day. It took all afternoon today to clear my head. I was so groggy. Every time I looked out the window of our wrecked plane at the mountainous granite walls, rocky outcroppings, and towering jack pines, all half-hidden behind a veil of blowing snow, I would think it was just a bad dream. But then I would look around at Pat and the boys, their faces filled with fear and concern, shivering in the frosty cabin, and I would realize again what had happened. But I don't remember the crash at all. All I know now is that my shoulder is separated and it is cold and cramped and I'm in pain.

But Pat is the most seriously hurt. "I think my back may be broken," she told me. The boys seem fine. They told me they went out yesterday to pack snow around a back cargo door that had sprung open. With the suitcases piled in front of the door, it makes a pretty good seal. It will keep some of the cold out. Against all odds, and because of Gary's skill when he belly flopped the plane into a snowbank, we have a pretty good capsule to survive in. For a while. There is no food; Christmas dinner tonight was a handful of snow. We are wearing only street clothes and light coats. Most of our ski clothes and equipment were shipped ahead. Only the boys have winter parkas and boots along.

I wonder if anybody else knows we have crashed? No matter. There's nothing for us to do but wait for somebody to find us—a white plane half-buried in snow.

Saturday. Last night was horrible! It came quickly and lingered long. Fifteen hours of the most overpowering blackness I have ever experienced. Every ten minutes I was looking at my watch, wondering when, if ever, the night would be over. Up here, the wind shrieks through the trees, a sound almost too painful to listen to. And it is cold—oh, so very cold. We slept only in fitful bursts. The rest of the time we talked a little and prayed for Gary, that he made it through safely. But did he? Then we just stared—into the heart of darkness.

It is snowing and blowing even harder and more furiously than yesterday. Arnie and Darren did venture out of the plane to look for Gary, but found nothing. Once I heard a distinct *crack!* and whirled around in my seat, only to see a branch had snapped off a nearby tree. The boys tried to use the wood to start a signal fire, but the wind kept blowing it out.

But what a moment today! Arnie was cleaning out his suitcase—he was going to fill it with snow for eating—when he found his Bible. I have never been that thrilled about a Bible before. But we all took turns reading favorite passages.

Our spirits are much higher tonight than this morning. I was even kidding the boys about our "gourmet" diet.

"What'll it be tonight?" I asked them.

"A pizza with pepperoni and bell peppers," ordered Arnie.

"Double cheeseburger, large order of fries, and a chocolate shake," Darren said.

And I reached out of the little window near me and grabbed a glob of snow. "Let's see, now," I said, holding out a snowball. "Which one of you gets the pizza?"

I've taken off my watch—looking at it makes the days last too long.

Sunday. As tired as I was last night, sleep still came only sporadically. Once I awoke with a start—I couldn't feel my body. It was numb all over. I panicked. Frantically I rubbed myself until the feeling finally came back. But when the feeling came back, so did the pain, especially in my shoulder. Finally, gritting my teeth, I yanked on the shoulder and, to my amazement, it popped back into place!

This morning I heard two planes fly overhead, but we couldn't see them. It's still snowing as fiercely as ever. Little things inside the plane tell me our time is slowly running out. I can feel it in the numbness of my feet. And the boys are becoming quieter. We don't joke about the snow anymore—in fact, we don't even eat it. Arnie discovered that the hoarfrost growing thicker and thicker on the inside walls of the cabin tastes better than snow. We use credit cards to scrape it off. We keep the window clear that way, too—we need that lifeline to the world.

Mostly, though, we just huddled close today. Arnie brought out his Bible and we read. How much like the psalmist we feel, crying out to God in the midst of our despair.

The boys, with their long but neatly kept brown hair, flashing dark eyes and endless energy, remind me all the time of Gary. If I dwell too much on him or friends or our situation, it becomes too much to bear, and I just have to weep, my whole body heaving with deep, wrenching sobs. It happens to all of us. Our remedy is to hug each other as tightly as we can. That simple touch seems to supply as much strength as it does warmth to a shivering body.

It's so cold, and hope is so hard to find.

Monday. I heard it shortly after daylight—a low throbbing sound in the distance. It was coming closer, its rhythmic *thub-thub-thub* unmistakable. A helicopter! Darren saw it first. As it got closer to us it slowed and then began descending to the bottom of the valley about a half-mile from the plane.

"They're landing! They've found us!" one of the boys shouted. How can I describe the joy that pulsed through each of us as we watched seven, eight, nine people jump out of the big, olive-green chopper and begin snowshoeing their way through the trees toward us? We were all hugging each other and thanking God, hollering and singing and carrying on in the best Texas tradition.

The big chopper flew off again as we excitedly squirmed in our cramped seats, waiting for the people to work their way up to us. We couldn't go out to meet them—chest-deep snow and frozen feet precluded that. "It sure is taking them a long time," Pat said. "Can we signal them somehow?" We yelled a little, but the wind was still too loud.

"It's getting dark," Darren said, and almost immediately the helicopter reappeared, coming over the mountain as it had that morning, settling down in that same spot in the same little valley, kicking up in the same snow. We watched with wide eyes as our rescue party began to reboard the chopper. We saw it all! Our desperate screams reached only our own ears. The helicopter lifted off and disappeared into the dusk. They hadn't seen us—they didn't even know we were here!

How can I explain the devastation we all felt? All we had been holding out for, hoping for, had been cruelly snatched away. We all broke into tears and sobbed. But finally, after about an hour, when the tears had stopped, Arnie pulled out his Bible and we read some more. How real it has become to us: "O my God, I cry by day, but thou dost not answer; and by night, but find no rest. Yet . . . in thee our fathers trusted; they trusted, and thou didst deliver them" (Psalm 22:3-4).

We *must* continue to trust, to wait for that deliverance.

Monday night. It's been the best and worst night of my entire life. All night long the wind has moaned eerily. None of us can sleep, at least not for long, and somebody has to be awake at all times to make sure Darren stays awake. His body temperature has dropped so dramatically that we are afraid we might lose him if we let him sleep. So we've been talking most of the time—sometimes praying, sometimes sharing the private concerns of our hearts. Tonight, we all prayed that God would do with us what he wanted. We have put our lives entirely in his hands now.

What a turning point that has been for me! Before the crash, I had gotten to the point in my life where I had quit praying. I didn't feel worthy or faithful enough to God to even approach him, when so often I had ignored him. I hated to reach out to God because that made me examine myself, and that hurt. But these last days I have known his presence. How alive those old Bible stories have become!

I'm the prodigal son of the parable, flawed, coming on my knees to ask of the barest essentials. I want that relationship with my Father again.

We talked a lot about faith tonight—what was our purpose here, why were there so many obstacles in life?

"Steve, what have you found?" Arnie asked me. "How do you get through hard times? And why, why are they there?"

"I don't know why we have them—they sure keep coming, don't they?" I said. "But I do know this. It seems that every time I have lived through a tough time, and stopped to look, I've learned something. Something good."

"What good has come from this, Steve?"

I marvel at the resilience of Arnie's spirit. His questions come from deep within, with no tinge of bitterness. He knows we are all slowly freezing to death, yet like the psalmist he is still grasping for that hope. I want so badly to give him that, to give him life. But that is not mine to do. "Arnie, I don't know what this means for you," I told him. "But tonight, when we prayed about putting our lives in God's hands, I experienced a peace I've never felt before. I discovered, *for sure,* that God will sustain me, no matter what. And that's good."

The warmth that has grown among us tonight has defied the bitter cold. As we talked, we opened up to one another in a way that affirmed the growing trust we are feeling, not only in God, but in each other. There were tears again, for a father and husband and friend we all know has been gone too long. For relationships, for friendship. But mostly they are tears of joy, for the blessing of God we are only now beginning to fully comprehend.

The moaning wind has stopped. And by morning peace has come to the mountains—and to us.

Tuesday. We were greeted this morning with streaks of sunlight, the first time since the crash. But there was no other sign of life, save two squirrels. It was quiet, peaceful, and very cold.

Pat was the first to repeat the question of last night. "Steve, why are we suffering like this? Why so much?" Her back is really hurting her, and, as with the rest of us, the cold has taken a severe toll.

I didn't know what to say. "Maybe Job will help," I finally answered. "Maybe now we can really understand what he has to say about suffering."

So Pat has been reading chapter after chapter; the rest of us have just stared at the window or made small talk. Last night really left us drained.

Pat just closed the Bible—I guess that means she is finished. It's a good thing too—already the sun has begun to slip down behind the high peaks. I wonder what she found, what she'll say about . . . wait! There's something coming down the hill. It's . . . it's a person, a man! Where did he come from? I didn't hear anything—no plane, no helicopter. Does he see us? Yes, yes he does! He's waving and shouting.

"Over here, over here!" There are more of them, two, three, four. They are running down the slope, from over the ridge. *Oh, God, thank you. You never forgot us, God, in five days here. You never left us. You never did—and I know you never will!*

A man's head pokes through the door of the cabin.

"Hi, folks," the man says, shaking the fluffy white coat of powder off his parka. "It's awful good to see you!"

The search for Steve, Pat, Arnie, and Darren—one of the largest in Colorado's history—had only resumed that Tuesday because of the sunshine. The previous night it was decided that rescuers would make one last-ditch effort to find the plane only if weather permitted. And when Ken Zahren, a medical student from Oregon who had volunteered to be a part of the search party, found the four, there was less than an hour of daylight left. The rescuers were shocked to find the four alive. Convinced that the group would be dead, the rescuers wept with joy, along with the survivors, at finding them.

Pat and the two boys were taken off the mountain that night in a helicopter, after the chopper pilot defied darkness and a new blizzard to land his craft on a wobbly boulder near the crash site. Near whiteout conditions finally forced him to take off before Steve and some rescuers could be loaded aboard. The next day, in a snowstorm, sixty people helped bring Steve down by sled—it took nine-and-a-half hours.

But this story of faith rediscovered and renewed doesn't end at the base of a mountain. It goes on, like faith itself, growing and developing, encouraging and sustaining. And if anyone ever needed a life-giving faith to endure, those four did.

Steve turned out to be the most seriously hurt. He had both legs amputated below the knee because of frostbite. Pat required back surgery for a fractured vertebrae, and both boys lost toes, also because of frostbite. For each, it was a long and difficult recovery, made more so because of the loss of Gary. His body was finally found in September after an intensive search. Yet the courage that faith gives, the knowledge that God was with them, remained alive and vital, brought healing of both body and spirit.

Today that faith lives stronger, deeper, more vibrant than ever in Steve and Pat and Arnie and Darren. "The crash was a new beginning for me," Steve says. "All that I went through was a small price to pay—for faith."

THIRTY-SEVEN

The Girl Who Was Frozen Solid

BY JEAN HILLIARD VIG
FOSSTON, MINNESOTA

She was going into town to meet some friends. She had no idea she'd be caught in a twenty-five-degrees-below-zero blizzard.

I grabbed my purse and the car keys, threw on my new green waist-length parka, and started toward the door. Mom called, "Jean, aren't you going to take your boots and snowmobile pants? It's supposed to get colder tonight."

I'd lived on a farm in northern Minnesota all my life and was used to cold weather. "I'll be fine, Mom. Just driving into town to meet some friends. It's not that cold."

I was nineteen years old and thought cowboy boots and blue jeans were more appropriate than warm clothing for a night out with friends. Besides, I had no idea that in just a few hours the temperature would plummet to twenty-five degrees below zero with gusts of fifty-mile-an-hour blizzard winds.

Around midnight, after a fun evening in Fosston with my friends, I was driving home in Dad's big white Ford LTD, I usually took the four-wheel-drive pickup, but tonight it was low on gas and Dad had said I could take the car.

Heading home, the snow sparkled festively in the beams of my headlights. I decided to take the old country gravel road because it was a few miles shorter than the blacktop. Besides, I had always loved that road. It meandered through a forest of tall pines. Every couple of miles a house or a farm dotted the landscape, but the rest was pure picture-postcard scenery—icy-blue Minnesota lakes, tall trees, and the narrow, winding, hilly gravel road.

I didn't see the small patch of ice in the middle of the road because of the new snow. Before I knew what was happening, the car skidded off to the side and the front wheel slid precariously close to the ditch. I tried to back up slowly, but the tires were spinning. When I put the car in forward gear the front tire slipped off the shoulder and the car became helplessly marooned.

I wasn't frightened, but I surely was disgusted! I could just hear Dad's booming voice when he found out what I had done with his good car.

I knew there was a house a half mile or so ahead, so I got out of the car, slammed the door, and stomped off down the road, forgetting my hat on the front seat.

I was steaming over the mess I had gotten myself into, and my anger kept me warm for a few hundred feet. The wind forced me to zip up my jacket collar over my nose and mouth. I shoved my hands deep into my pockets and dug into the snow in my pointy-toed leather cowboy boots.

I walked on a little farther and then remembered Wally's place, in the opposite direction. *It should be just a half mile, or so,* I thought. Wally was an acquaintance of my folks and I knew he had a four-wheel-drive truck and could pull my car out of the ditch easily.

As I passed the car, I felt like kicking the tire, but I trudged on. After a half mile or so, I passed a house. It was dark and there were no tracks in the driveway. *Probably out of town,* I thought.

I walked on another half mile or more. The next house was also dark and the driveway filled with snow without a tire track to be seen. (I found out later that both of these families *were* home that night and that the wind had blown the snow over all the tracks an hour or so before I became stranded.)

I pressed on. The wind whipped and whistled through the pines. My feet were starting to bother me. My dressy high-heeled cowboy boots were not meant for hiking. *Why had I taken the shortcut? At least on the blacktop there would be cars on the road this time of night.*

I struggled up another hill. Finally, I thought I saw Wally's farm in the distance. Yes! There was the long lane leading to his house. I was breathing harder. And then . . . I blanked out.

Although I don't remember it, apparently I half-walked, half-stumbled, falling at times, down that long lane. I crawled the last hundred feet or so on my hands and knees, but I don't remember doing that either.

By now, the wind chill factor was seventy to eighty degrees below zero. Right at Wally's front door I collapsed and fell face forward into the snow. And that's where I lay all night.

The next morning Wally came out his front door just before seven o'clock. Normally he didn't go to work until eight but, thank God, he decided to go in early that morning. Wally saw my body in the snow, leaned down and tried to find a pulse. There was none. My swollen face was a gray, ashen color. My eyes were frozen open. I wasn't breathing.

Wally still doesn't know how he managed to pick me up and get me into his car. He said it was like struggling with a 120-pound cordwood stick or a big piece of meat out of the freezer.

At the hospital in Fosston, Wally yelled through the emergency room doorway for help. He picked me up under my arms and a couple of nurses lifted my ankles. My body didn't bend anywhere.

As they were putting me on a stretcher, one nurse exclaimed, "She's frozen solid!" Another nurse, the mother of one of my best friends, said, "I think it's Jean Hilliard! I recognize her blond hair and the green jacket!"

Mrs. Rosie Erickson, who works in bookkeeping, ran out in the hall when she heard the commotion. She leaned over my body. "Wait! Listen!" A hush fell around my stretcher. "It's a moaning sound . . . coming from her throat! Listen!"

I was wheeled into the emergency room. Dr. George Sather, our family doctor, was on duty that morning. He was unable to hear any breathing or a heartbeat with his stethoscope. Then he attached a heart monitor, which picked up a very slow, faint heartbeat. A cardiologist said it seemed to be "a dying heart."

"We have to get these boots off! Bring some blankets! She's still alive!" The emergency room sprang to life. My boots and jacket were the only clothing items they could get off immediately. The rest of my clothes were frozen on me.

When they cut my jeans off, the staff saw that my feet were black and there were black areas on my legs and lower back. My feet and legs were swollen. The tissue damage seemed so severe that when my parents arrived, Dr. Sather told them that if I *did* live, my legs might have to be amputated. He wanted my parents to be prepared.

Dr. Sather ordered oxygen, and a nurse suggested trying "Aqua-K-pads." Just the day before, a new kind of water-filled heating pad had arrived at the hospital. Quickly the nurses unpacked one heating pad box after another. Fortunately, the only nurse on the staff who knew how to connect them to the special water-filled machines was on duty and she directed the operation.

My body was frozen so hard that they couldn't pierce my skin with a hypodermic needle. There was no way at first to give me any medication to speed the thawing process or to prevent infection. But the medical team didn't know what Rosie Erickson was about to do.

Rosie found my parents in the hall. "Mr. and Mrs. Hilliard, do you mind if I put Jean on the prayer chain at our church?"

Mom, who was completely bewildered at the scene before her, answered, quickly, "Yes, please do!"

Mrs. Erickson hurried to her office and made a phone call to the prayer chain chairman at the Baptist church where her husband is pastor. The prayer chain was set in motion. The first person on the list called the second. That person called the third and so on.

My heart started beating slightly faster. Even though still far slower than the normal rate of about seventy-two times a minute, the doctors were overjoyed. Slowly I started breathing on my own.

The prayer chain was lengthening. Mrs. Erickson called the pastors of the Lutheran, Catholic, Methodist, and Bethel Assembly churches in Fosston. They, in turn, called the chairmen of their prayer chain groups, who passed the word along.

During the first hours that the prayer chain was underway, my legs and feet, instead of getting darker as Dr. Sather expected, started to lighten and regain their natural color. One after another, the doctors and nurses filed in to marvel at the pinkish tinge appearing at the line of demarcation where the darkness started. (That was the line on my upper thighs where Dr. Sather said he thought they might have to amputate.)

The prayer chain spread to the nearby towns of Crookston and

Bemidji, and Grand Forks, North Dakota. Soon hundreds, then thousands of people were aware that a young woman had been brought in to the Fosston hospital frozen solid and was in desperate need of God's miraculous healing.

One of the nurses, on her way to get more blankets, poked her head into Mrs. Erickson's doorway and said, "She might make it! Her legs are starting to regain color at the top! And her heart is beating stronger!"

Mrs. Erickson looked up at the clock and thought, *The prayer chain is in full swing now. God is answering those prayers already. Of course she's going to make it!*

At that moment the whole attitude in my hospital room changed. Now, instead of "She probably won't survive," the feeling was "Perhaps she'll live, but she will surely lose her legs from the knees down."

Before noon that day, I stirred and moaned a word that sounded like "Mom." My mother and oldest sister Sandra stayed near my bed, holding, squeezing, and patting my hands. "Jean, Jean, wake up! Jeannie, can you hear me? It's Mom. Sandra's here too. Jeannie, we love you. Jeannie, can you hear?" Around noon I mumbled a few words to them.

All over the area the prayer chain was continuing.

By midafternoon I woke up and started thrashing in bed. The doctors told me later that I moaned and yelled so much that they were convinced I would have severe brain damage.

All day the nurses and doctors watched in amazement as the blackness in my legs and feet disappeared inch by inch.

By late afternoon Dr. Sather thought perhaps my legs would be saved and that only my feet might have to be amputated. A few hours later he was astounded to realize that perhaps it would be just my toes.

In the end I did not lose any part of my body! Normal color and circulation came back to even the blackest parts of my legs, feet, and toes.

Dr. Sather had also thought he would have to do numerous skin grafts where huge blisters covered my toes. But these places healed too without skin grafting.

Indeed, after watching my body become whole again, I am convinced that a miracle did occur. Even Dr. Sather said, "I just took care of her. God healed her."

The doctors kept me in the hospital seven weeks to make sure of my recovery from frostbite and to lessen the possibility of any infection in my toes. And that entire time I never once experienced any fear. I am convinced it was the prayer chain that kept me calm and filled me with a positive faith that I would be healed.

The night I nearly froze to death was more than seven years ago—December 20, 1980. Since then I met a wonderful man, got married, and had two beautiful children. My husband, children, and I live on a farm outside Fosston, and my life is a tranquil, happy one. But there isn't a day that goes by that I don't think about the night I nearly froze to death.

I've become a different person because of that experience. Last winter, I joined forces with a civil defense expert, an army sergeant, a highway patrolman, and a doctor from Crookston who is an expert in hypothermia (subnormal body temperature). We give talks to people in different towns and counties around here about winter survival. I tell them my story and point out what can happen when you go out in the winter unprepared for the weather.

I am surprised I can do this because when I was in high school I was absolutely terrified of speech class. The thought of standing in front of people with all eyes on me almost made me sick to my stomach. But now I feel none of that. I am proud to share my story with the hope that I can help even one person avoid the mistakes I made.

I believe this is the reason God spared me—so that I can help other people learn how to survive the changeable and very cold winters.

I've changed in other ways too. My family and I are much closer now. I appreciate every day I'm alive. I have an enormous respect for the power of prayer. I believe that the prayer chains saved my life. Thousands of people I didn't even know bombarded heaven with powerful prayer requests in my behalf, and against all medical odds I survived. I not only lived, I survived as a completely normal, whole human being without even so much as a skin graft. In fact, unlike most other people who have suffered from frostbite, I now experience no ill effects from the cold.

As one minister reminded me in the hospital when we spoke of the prayer chain, we, as God's children have been commanded to "Pray without ceasing" (1 Thessalonians 5:17).

And I am sure that was what caused my miracle—all those people praying unceasingly for me.

THIRTY-EIGHT

"Hang On! We'll Get You Out!"

BY ROBERT EBELING
DIETERICH, ILLINOIS

There was something ominous about the giant smokestack looming over us that cloudy September morning in 1977. In all my thirty-three years I had never worked inside a thing like that.

Towering 650 feet, its top scraped the muddy cumulus clouds that rolled across the gray sky. A thunderstorm was expected. *The last thing we need,* I thought. The job was dangerous enough without the threat of rain and high winds. But Bob Silvers, a burly forty-five-year-old construction worker from Kansas City, had worked on smokestack jobs before and seemed confident.

He and I had been hired by Gunite Construction Company to apply a sealer coat to the inner liner of *Columbia II,* which is what the Wisconsin Power and Light Plant of Portage, Wisconsin, called this main stack.

It was hazardous work, but the money was important to me. Pam and I and our three-year-old son lived in a nice house in a good neighborhood. We were a steady, churchgoing family, and I was proud of my ability to provide for them.

As we stepped inside the damp, echoing sixty-foot-wide base and I peered up through sixty-five stories of black tubing with a bull's-eye view of the sky, icy tingles raced up my spine. But I felt better when I saw the sturdy, well-designed scaffold on which we would work. The frame was made of four aluminum beams overlaid with two-by-twelve-inch oak boards forming a substantial platform.

Four steel cables soared to the top of the stack. Attached to each cable at the platform's corners was a small electric motor that would power our ascent and descent.

Bob and I stepped onto the platform. Black walls of the liner slipped past and the small circle of light above widened until finally we reached the top, which had narrowed to twenty-two feet in diameter. I took a moment to peer down at the hazy countryside dotted with tiny houses and buglike cars. Tall lightning rods sprouted from the mouth of the stack, which was ringed by a narrow catwalk. My coveralls snapped in the wind.

"Time to get to work, buddy," laughed Silvers. "Got to beat that storm."

By 6:00 P.M. that day, we had sprayed the thick black sealer about 250 feet down. We had another twenty minutes to work when I switched on a motor to level my edge of the platform down ten inches. The corner of the scaffold glided down, but the motor wouldn't switch off! I frantically flipped the switch on and off. I beat it and cursed it. But the humming motor wouldn't stop! The scaffold dipped to a sickening thirty-degree pitch; a big drum of sealer skidded across, slid off the edge and crashed 400 feet below with a hollow boom. Silvers was yelling. The platform sank further. The oaken boards were sliding!

Struggling to the high side of the platform, I screamed into the intercom that a motor wouldn't shut off. Silvers was bellowing. "Cut the power! Cut the power!" But the foreman below didn't seem to understand what was happening.

As more boards slid off the aluminum frame, Bob and I each lunged for a cable. The oily braided steel did not afford much grip, but by wrapping our legs around it and using all our strength, we found that we could support ourselves.

Finally the motor's power was cut and the foreman shouted up: "I'll get help!"

The platform, which I once had thought was so secure, now dangled crazily, creaking from its own weight.

For an endless hour we hung above forty stories of emptiness. Every so often someone at the base of the stack would yell, "Don't worry. We'll get you!" But nothing happened.

Time dragged on with excruciating slowness.

"God in heaven," I cried, "where is everybody?" My arms became numb. My muscles ached. And every five minutes or so, up would float a faint voice assuring us that help was on the way.

Three hours passed as we clung to the cables like monkeys on a string. Every fiber of my body cried out with pain and exhaustion. I thought how simple it would be to just let go and fall into the velvety blackness.

Today was Pam's birthday. I had promised to call her. She would be waiting.

My legs seemed paralyzed. Could I ever straighten my fingers? Silvers, his voice hoarse from yelling, was begging someone to hurry. I felt my grip slipping.

"God help us," I moaned. "I can't hold on any longer."

Sharp metal slivers stung my hands as I slipped down helplessly. Suddenly my feet struck a projection on the cable. The motor! It gave some support. "Slide down to the motor," I told Silvers. "It helps a little."

Another hour passed. On the ground outside milled a crowd of ironworkers and townspeople, including the fire chief, sheriff, and plant superintendent. No one knew what to do. It was finally decided to let a big bucket down to us from the top. But how? And with what?

Someone thought of a helicopter and called the Air National Guard. But Bob and I didn't know this. All we heard was an occasional faint call assuring us. "Hold on; we'll get you out!"

"But we've been here over five hours!" I cried in desperation.

Now it was midnight. My throat was parched. It had been twelve hours since we had had food or water. A cold wind moaned up the clammy stack. My flesh tightened and I shivered.

"I can't stand this any longer," I cried.

"You'd better!" Silvers said grimly, adding, "All we can do now is pray."

Suddenly there was a beating sound through the wind. A helicopter, right over us! We strained to see tiny, winking lights against the black sky. It hovered, went away, then all was quiet.

We didn't know that it was a private helicopter attempting to lower a basket to us. But by what miracle could a chopper lower a basket—spinning crazily in the wind—in the black of night into a twenty-two-foot-wide opening that the pilot couldn't even see?

Thunder rumbled, echoing up and down our vertical tunnel, and the sky lit up through the bull's-eye above. Then rain slashed us in long strings of needle-sharp ice. I thirstily licked it off my face, but it chilled me to the bone as it soaked through my coveralls.

"For God's sake," I screamed into the wind, "Somebody help us!" Again came the faint shout that help was coming.

Then all was quiet. And in the deathly stillness, I suddenly knew. No help was coming. Everything I had placed my trust in had failed; the scaffold that seemed so solid, the men working below, even the helicopter that had come and gone.

There in that towering tomb I realized that there is nothing or no one in this world on which we can place our complete dependence. Machines can malfunction; people can fail. Only our Creator is for sure.

How many times had I used God's name these past terrible hours? Yet, as surely as I hung there, I knew I had been using it as a charm, a talisman, like knocking on wood for luck. It had been like my church-going these past years, a mechanical habit.

In losing every worldly support and hanging helpless before death, truth became clear to me. I knew that God wasn't just a name, but a living Person who had told us that no matter where we would be, in the uttermost parts of the earth or trapped in a sixty-five-story smoke-stack, he would be with us.

It was then I felt his presence, surrounding me, comforting me. My hysteria and panic subsided. My muscles still ached, and I was freezing. But I had lost much of my fear.

Then the intercom crackled: "We've got an Air National Guard helicopter coming in."

Finally we heard the chopping overhead. For an instant we saw winking lights, but then they blurred and disappeared. Fog! Fog was rolling in! The chopping noise disappeared. The intercom explained that the wind was too fierce and the fog too thick for the pilot to stabilize over the stack. Moreover, the fog-enshrouded lightning rods were a hazard.

My heart sank. Then the voice on the intercom added that a big Chinook helicopter was on its way. Earlier, five men had been lifted to the catwalk at the top of the stack by a helicopter. They had carried nylon band slings bound to their chests. These would be lowered to us so that if the entire platform fell we would have some support.

Soon the slings were fed slowly down the 250 feet. We were told to slip into them and not worry if the platform went; the straps might stretch twenty feet but would hold. *Twenty feet?*

Now it was 1:00 A.M. Wind sucked at our water-soaked clothing.

"Dear Lord," I whispered, "I know that you are a mighty help in time of trouble. Thank you for being here."

The mighty beating of the Chinook now resounded through the stack and our spirits soared, only to crash again when told that the pilot found it too difficult to maneuver in the strong wind.

"Oh, Father, help us to hold on," I prayed.

At 4:00 A.M. the intercom came alive to tell us that two Coast Guard helicopters had arrived. "They have more sophisticated rescue equipment," we were told. Then we heard one, but saw nothing.

A subdued intercom voice explained that the pilot was not only fighting fog, wind, darkness, and tall, invisible spikes, but once again was trying to drop a metal bucket-cage that was being whipped around crazily by the wind into a very small opening.

"Rescue is impossible now," the voice continued. "We must wait until the wind dies and the fog lifts, maybe by daybreak. . . ."

For a long time it was silent. Only the wind boomed through the steel tube. Suddenly, again a chopper's beating. We didn't know that in a last desperate attempt the Coast Guard chopper had somehow lowered the wind-whirled bucket to the men on the catwalk. They had miraculously caught it, and were able to guide it into the stack.

There was a sudden banging of metal, and we squinted up to see the basket, looking like a tiny dot, descending in the dim light. As it swung in circles between us, I caught it, then realized the metal cage could hold only one person. It was two feet square and five feet high.

"Get in!" ordered Silvers. "I've been with the company eighteen years and have been through more hassles than you have. They'll get me right away."

Somehow I managed to open the door of the wobbly cage. Weak and shaking, I squeezed my stiff body inside, then sobbed out, "Ready!"

The cage lifted like a wild elevator.

"Dear God, thank you!" I gasped. "I'm going up, getting out!" I could hear the helicopter laboring against the wind. Suddenly the basket shuddered, hesitated, and began falling. As it neared the platform, I shut my eyes, fearing the blow would send the platform to the bottom.

Then the basket jerked up again and we seemed to fly . . . forty feet . . . sixty . . . eighty. . . . But again it stopped and again we dropped sickeningly.

"Oh, God," I prayed, "help Silvers." Again we were climbing, the cage spinning like a top, crashing into the steel sides of the liner. Suddenly I was outside, and there was the whole wide sky!

Tears streamed down my face as the basket, now swinging in a 200-foot circle like a runaway carnival ride, began settling to the earth. Then we crashed heavily on the rain-soaked ground. Metal dug into my knees and mud oozed up into the cage. Sweet cool mud. Someone helped me onto a stretcher and into an ambulance. As it rushed me to Devine Hospital, I prayed for Silvers, hoping they would soon get him out. We had been trapped in that stack nineteen hours without food or water.

When I awakened in the hospital, it was late morning. I learned that the weather had turned too severe for another basket rescue. Silvers was still in the stack, and my heart ached with fear for him.

I leaned forward in my bed and through the window could see dark Columbia II towering in the distance. Helicopters, looking like dragonflies, hovered around it.

I prayed that the Lord would sustain my friend. Somehow I felt that the Lord was with Silvers, and that he would come out all right.

The biggest lesson I learned in those nineteen awful hours was where to put my trust—in God, our Father, and his Son, Jesus Christ.

Editor's note: Bob Silvers was finally rescued at 11:40 that morning. Lt. Rick Hauschildt and his copilot, Jeff Kaylor, described the two rescues as the most difficult and frightening mission of their lives.

THIRTY-NINE

An Exchange of Gifts

BY DIANE RAYNER
BELLEVUE, WASHINGTON

I grew up believing that Christmas was a time when strange and wonderful things happened, when wise and royal visitors came riding, when at midnight the barnyard animals talked to one another, and in the light of a fabulous star God came down to us as a little Child. Christmas to me has always been a time of enchantment, and never more so than the year that my son Marty was eight.

That was the year that my children and I moved into a cozy trailer home in a forested area just outside of Redmond, Washington. As the holiday approached, our spirits were light, not to be dampened even by the winter rains that swept down Puget Sound to douse our home and make our floors muddy.

Throughout that December, Marty had been the most spirited, and busiest, of us all. He was my youngest, a cheerful boy, blond-haired and playful, with a quaint habit of looking up at you and cocking his head like a puppy when you talked to him. Actually, the reason for this was that Marty was deaf in his left ear, but it was a condition that he never complained about.

For weeks I had been watching Marty. I knew that something was going on with him that he was not telling me about. I saw how *eagerly* he made his bed, took out the trash, and *carefully* set the table and helped Rick and Pam prepare dinner before I got home from work. I saw how he silently collected his tiny allowance and tucked it away, spending not a cent of it. I had no idea what all this quiet activity was about, but I suspected that somehow it had something to do with Kenny.

Kenny was Marty's friend, and ever since they had found each other in the springtime, they were seldom apart. If you called to one, you got them both. Their world was in the meadow, a horse pasture broken by a small winding stream, where the boys caught frogs and snakes, where they would search for arrowheads or hidden treasure, or where they would spend an afternoon feeding peanuts to the squirrels.

Times were hard for our little family, and we had to do some scrimping to get by. With my job as a meat wrapper and with a lot of ingenuity around the trailer, we managed to have elegance on a shoestring. But not Kenny's family. They were desperately poor, and his mother was having a real struggle to feed and clothe her two children. They were a good, solid family. But Kenny's mom was a proud woman, very proud, and she had strict rules.

How we worked, as we did each year, to make our home festive for the holiday! Ours was a handcrafted Christmas of gifts hidden away and ornaments strung about the place.

Marty and Kenny would sometimes sit still at the table long enough to help make cornucopias or weave little baskets for the tree. But then, in a flash, one would whisper to the other, and they would be out the door and sliding cautiously under the electric fence into the horse pasture that separated our home from Kenny's.

One night shortly before Christmas, when my hands were deep in *Peppernoder* dough, shaping tiny nutlike Danish cookies heavily spiced with cinnamon, Marty came to me and said in a tone mixed with pleasure and pride, "Mom, I've bought Kenny a Christmas present. Want to see it?" *So that's what he's been up to,* I said to myself. "It's something he's wanted for a long, long time, Mom."

After carefully wiping his hands on a dish towel, he pulled from his pocket a small box. Lifting the lid, I gazed at the pocket compass that my son had been saving all those allowances to buy. A little compass to point an eight-year-old adventurer through the woods.

"It's a lovely gift, Martin," I said, but even as I spoke, a disturbing thought came to mind. I knew how Kenny's mother felt about their poverty. They could barely afford to exchange gifts among themselves, and giving presents to others was out of the question. I was sure that Kenny's proud mother would not permit her son to receive something he could not return in kind.

Gently, carefully, I talked over the problem with Marty. He understood what I was saying.

"I know, Mom, I *know!* . . . But what if it was a *secret?* What if they never found out *who* gave it?"

I didn't know how to answer him. I just didn't know.

The day before Christmas was rainy and cold and gray. The three kids and I all but fell over one another as we elbowed our way about our little home putting finishing touches on Christmas secrets and preparing for family and friends who would be dropping by.

Night settled in. The rain continued. I looked out the window over the sink and felt an odd sadness. How mundane the rain seemed for a Christmas Eve! Would wise and royal men come riding on such a night? I doubted it. It seemed to me that strange and wonderful things happened only on clear nights, nights when one could at least see a star in the heavens.

I turned from the window, and as I checked on the ham and lefse bread warming in the oven, I saw Marty slip out the door. He wore his coat over his pajamas, and he clutched a tiny, colorfully wrapped box in his pocket.

Down through the soggy pasture he went, then a quick slide under the electric fence and across the yard to Kenny's house. Up the steps on tiptoe, shoes squishing; open the screen door just a crack; place the gift on the doorstep, then a deep breath, a reach for the doorbell, and a press on it *hard.*

Quickly Marty turned, ran down the steps and across the yard in a wild race to get away unnoticed. Then, suddenly, he banged into the electric fence.

The shock sent him reeling. He lay stunned on the wet ground. His body quivered and he gasped for breath. Then slowly, weakly, confused and frightened, he began the grueling trip back home.

"Marty," we cried as he stumbled through the door, "what happened?" His lower lip quivered, his eyes brimmed.

"I forgot about the fence, and it knocked me down!"

I hugged his muddy little body to me. He was still dazed, and there was a red mark beginning to blister on his face from his mouth to his ear. Quickly I treated the blister and, with a warm cup of cocoa soothing him, Marty's bright spirits returned. I tucked him into bed and just before he fell asleep he looked up at me and said, "Mom, Kenny didn't see me. I'm sure he didn't see me."

That Christmas Eve I went to bed unhappy and puzzled. It seemed such a cruel thing to happen to a little boy while on the purest kind of Christmas mission, doing what the Lord wants us all to do—giving to others—and giving in secret at that. I did not sleep well that night. Somewhere deep inside I think I must have been feeling the disappointment that the night of Christmas had come and it had been just an ordinary, problem-filled night, no mysterious enchantment at all.

But I was wrong.

By morning the rain had stopped and the sun shone. The streak on Marty's face was very red, but I could tell that the burn was not serious. We opened our presents, and soon, not unexpectedly, Kenny was knocking on the door, eager to show Marty his new compass and tell about the mystery of its arrival. It was plain that Kenny didn't suspect Marty at all, and while the two of them talked, Marty just smiled and smiled.

Then I noticed that while the two boys were comparing their Christmases, nodding and gesturing and chattering away, Marty was not cocking his head. When Kenny was talking, Marty seemed to be listening with his deaf ear. Weeks later a report came from the school nurse, verifying what Marty and I already knew. "Marty now has complete hearing in *both ears*."

The mystery of how Marty regained his hearing, and still has it, remains just that—a mystery. Doctors suspect, of course, that the shock from the electric fence was somehow responsible. Perhaps so. Whatever the reason, I just remain thankful to God for the good exchange of gifts that was made that night.

So you see, strange and wonderful things still happen on the night of our Lord's birth. And one does not have to have a clear night, either, to follow a fabulous star.

FORTY

God, Let Me Raise My Kids!

BY BETTY CUSACK
BRONX, NEW YORK

I was tired, but I felt like rejoicing. With five children to support all by myself since I lost my husband, God had helped me find a job, and he was helping me raise up my children for a better life. He was good.

I was returning home when I pulled off the busy Cross Bronx Expressway and drove slowly up Boone Avenue to the top of the hill.

It was a cold morning in February 1974. As I reached the top of the hill, I stopped and stared in surprise at the ice-coated cobblestone street. Then the car behind me banged into me, and over the crest I went. The car behind slid over, too.

Sliding down the icy hill was like playing a terrifying game of bumper cars. I careened from one side of the street to the other, hitting parked automobiles. My car spun around and around while faster-moving cars came over the top of the hill and crashed into me. First one hit me, then another. And another. In all, five cars smashed into mine, which finally came to rest at the bottom of the hill, battered and caved in.

I heard glass crash as I tasted blood. I gripped the steering wheel and, thinking of my five children with no father, I prayed, "Dear God, all I want to do is raise my children. Then I'll be ready to go!"

I must have gone blank after that. When I came to, I was the only one around in all the wreckage. An onlooker came by and said that an ambulance had come and taken all it could. It didn't take me because the crew thought I was dead and they only had room for the living.

I'm alive! I thought. *I'm alive!* I snapped my fingers joyfully to prove it. *Oh, Lord, thank you for hearing my prayer!*

God gave me the strength to get up out of that crushed heap and walk home through the snow. I didn't even know I was hurt. I just kept repeating to myself, "Got to fix supper for the kids." I was in shock, I realize now. I should have stayed for the next ambulance or police car.

It was only the next day, telling my sister about the accident over the telephone, that I started to feel peculiar.

"Come get me!" I gasped. "I'm going numb!"

By the time she arrived, I couldn't move any of the left side of my body. When we got to the hospital, I couldn't talk.

Doctors and nurses stood over me. They said my neck was broken, my spine damaged. They said my intestines were ruptured and bleeding inside, and all the muscles were damaged on the left side of my body.

"Dear Lord," I wanted to shout. "I feel too good inside to be dying. Tell them for me, please."

But I lay there silenced for two days, and nothing changed. People buzzed around me. I heard them say I might not make it. I heard them say I would never talk or walk again. Finally, the reality of it hit me. And something like despair. I had learned to accept a lot of things in my life, even my husband's death. But God didn't make me a quitter. When I lost Cleveland, I prayed, "Lord, I don't have a penny. Guess you'll have to show me how to raise these children the way you want." And he did. I was praying again now. I couldn't talk, so God was the only One who could hear me. He always does.

"If I have to live like this, take me away now. But I know you want me to raise my kids up good. I'm not quitting on you yet, Lord."

Then I noticed a doctor pointing at me. I heard his words: "This one's amazing, walked for miles with a broken neck."

Yes, I thought. *When God helped me then, he was sending me a message. "Betty," he was saying, "you can pull through this, too."*

The next day people hovered about again, bemoaning what a shame it was that I would never recover. Maybe they didn't know the kind of God I had. I felt I had to contradict them or I would burst. My face got red, my jaw got tight, my mouth opened—and words came out!

Now they were all speechless—and even more so when I forced the words out: "I'm going back to work." I had to, I was raising God's children.

Right after my husband died in 1969, when my youngest was just an infant, I had to work steadily. It was hard for me to find a good job and just as hard to find baby-sitters. Then one day, when I was home from work and felt like giving up, I started praying for an answer, and a lady from Stanley Home Products rang my bell to recruit me to give product demonstrations in people's homes.

"Maybe you can help me . . . ," she began.

"Maybe you can help *me,*" I answered as I showed her in. *My,* I thought, *the Lord acts quickly.* This was work I could do on my own time or even with my kids. I started right away and by the time of the accident had sold my way up to Unit Sales Leader.

Now I was in trouble again! "Lord, I'm always in trouble," I prayed. "How am I going to earn a living from a hospital bed?"

Well, the answer sort of came: *I gave you one job; how many do you want?* So I started in right away selling from my hospital bed. After all, the Lord let me raise my children, so I had to get on with it. Though my Momma was staying with them, someone still had to support them.

And why had God given me my voice back? Why, so I could sell!

All the managers from Stanley trooped in to visit me, bringing creams and lotions and soap. I set up displays at my bedside and sold to visitors, doctors, and nurses. Then I thought, *Why should I stay in this nice semiprivate room, which costs so much, when in the ward there are twelve patients, each with their visitors, doctors, and nurses?* I got myself transferred right then and there. I passed catalogs around. I demonstrated the all-purpose cream, rubbing my good right hand against my useless left hand. Soon I was making almost as much money as before.

"Lord," I said, "I'm grateful for what you've done for me, but please, Lord, I don't want just to support my kids. I want to raise them. I've got to get out of this hospital. I've got to walk!"

The doctors were still saying I wouldn't walk, but they just made me mad. "Who are you to tell me I can't walk?" I fumed. "Are you my Master? I've already got One who says I can walk."

This was about a month after the accident. That day when the attendant helped me into a wheelchair for my trip to the X-ray room, I rebelled.

"Take this thing away," I ordered. "I'm going to walk."

The attendant's mouth fell open. The nurse said, "Now, Betty . . ."

But I just closed my eyes and pushed myself to the edge of the chair. "Please, God," I prayed. "Let me walk now."

I pushed up with my good right arm till I was on my feet. I was dizzy at being so high. I swayed, but managed to push against the wall for support. The nurse and attendant hovered anxiously.

"Betty, won't you sit. . . ."

I shook my head fiercely. "Please, God," I whispered. "You didn't make me a quitter." I took my hands off the wall and balanced. Everyone in the ward was staring at me now. There wasn't a sound. I put my right foot out and held my breath. Then I dragged my left foot forward in front of my right. The pain was terrible, but I stood there.

Then I collapsed in a heap.

"Thank you, Lord!" I whispered. "I knew you could do it." I had taken my first step.

In the next few days I took more and more steps. My legs were moving slowly, but they were moving! Then the doctors gave me a neck brace to gain control of my head. And just three months after the accident, I was out of that hospital and home with my kids. After we hugged and kissed and cried, the first thing I saw was a mountain of cartons on the living room floor—Stanley Products waiting to be sold.

"Lord," I said, "you don't let up, do you? I see what I have to do."

I started right away, neck brace and all. I arranged demonstrations at people's homes. My kids helped me carry the boxes. I laughed and kidded when I sold, and people helped me. I believe that if you look right into someone's eyes and ask for help, you will get it.

I wore that neck brace for four years. Lots of mornings it was a challenge just to roll out of bed, but I said to myself, "Betty, if the Lord could do all he's done for you, the least you can do is get this body of yours out of bed." And I did.

The pain never left me, but I refused to give in to it. I was as good a mother as I knew how, and I sold up a storm.

Then three years ago I got married to a wonderful man. In 1978, about the time my brace was finally removed, Stanley promoted me to District Sales Manger, with twenty-eight people in my district.

Now when they come to me unhappy or discouraged with life and feel they can't go on, I tell them, "Now look here. The only way you can be defeated is to quit on life. Life never quits on you. But just living isn't enough. You've got to put in time with God too.

"Without him, I'd still be lying in that hospital bed—no voice, unable to walk—feeling sorry for myself. With his help, I have my legs back, and I have my voice. Now I can walk and work and sing thanks for all his blessings."

I'm alive! And I'm not quitting!

FORTY-ONE

Hidden Danger

BY S. RICHARD PASTORELLA
NEW YORK CITY DETECTIVE

It's one of the most perilous of all jobs—
the police bomb squad.

"Thank you, Lord, for giving me the blessing of your strength to meet the challenges of the day."

That was the prayer I said to God every day from my teenage years right up until I reached the age of forty-two. Then I stopped saying that prayer. Or any prayers at all. I felt that God had dealt me a cruel, undeserved blow. I believed that my life was over.

I had been devoted to God while growing up. From childhood on my parents instilled in me their own love and trust in the Creator. One of my cherished memories is that of my father, a construction worker, awed by a splendid sunset, sweeping his eyes across the cloudless sky, and instinctively genuflecting. We were that kind of family. Loving. Trusting.

And that is the kind of family I wanted my own to be when Mary and I were married and as our two boys, Richard and Mark, came along. By then I was a member of the New York City Police Department. Eager to get to the top, I earned ten decorations, was promoted to detective, and in 1981, I made a major career decision. I volunteered for the police bomb squad.

"Why?" Mary asked me over and over again. "Why?"

I tried to explain. "Every policeman faces unknown danger every minute," I said, and I reminded her of all the times I had skirted death. "Bomb squad work is dangerous, yes, but it is a *known* danger. I trust my instinct, my skill." I didn't have to add that I trusted God.

During my first eighteen months in the bomb squad, I was out on about seventy-five calls, most of them to collect big caches of illegal, dangerous fireworks, or to do an investigation after a bomb exploded.

Then came New Year's Eve 1982.

At bomb squad headquarters, my partner, Tony Senft, and I munched cookies and gabbed. The phone had been silent since our shift had begun at 3:00 P.M.

It was now 9:20 P.M. We were certain the rest of the night would be quiet.

At 9:25 we were rushing out of the building with High Hat, the squad's German shepherd. At top speed, sirens whining, we drove to the plaza of a federal building in downtown Manhattan. A bomb had exploded. No one was injured. We examined the debris of the bomb and were checking for other bombs when word was flashed that another explosive had gone off at police headquarters three blocks away. We rushed over. There, lying on the ground, was a police officer: Rocco Pascarella, bloodied but conscious. I bent over Rocco.

"What did the bomb look like?" I asked. I had to ask because I knew that very likely there were other bombs around.

"In . . . in a . . . in a bag." His words came in painful gasps. "Bag . . . like . . . Chicken Delight." He started to raise himself on his elbow. Quickly I draped the bottom of my coat over him. I didn't want him to see that one of his legs was gone.

The ambulance crew arrived, lifted him gently onto a stretcher, and wheeled him away. Tony and I bowed our heads in a silent prayer for Rocco and turned immediately to check the street level around headquarters. High Hat began sniffing the area. He was trained to sit down if his nose detected explosives.

The dog pulled Tony toward two support columns. Two paper bags lay behind him. High Hat sat down.

Two bombs had already gone off. There might be two more ready to go off in those paper bags. We needed more bomb squad men. Tony went off to phone. A radio signal could trigger a live bomb.

Passersby began to collect. I asked the uniformed policemen at the scene to move them and High Hat behind a wall thirty feet away. Tony returned and stationed himself behind me. Carefully I prepared to remove a bomb blanket which had been placed around the suspected device. Instinctively, I clutched a religious medal in my pocket with my left hand while I moved my right hand toward the first bag.

That is all I remember.

I woke up in a hospital bed on New Year's Day, my head entirely bandaged, a roar in both ears, and a pain so unbearable I had to choke back a scream.

Even in my agony I felt that all this would pass. I would be OK. God would see to that.

A week later I learned of the lives the bombs had shattered. Rocco had lost not only a leg, but the sight of one eye and a lot of his hearing. Tony lost an eye and much of his hearing. My face and right arm were badly burned. I had only stumps of fingers on my right hand, no hearing in my right ear, very little in my left; one eye had been removed and I was blind in the other. My police career was over. I wasn't much use to anybody. Why had God abandoned me?

Even a surprising phone call from President Reagan could not diminish my bitterness.

"Nancy and I are praying for you," the President said. "You've suffered a terrible tragedy, but I'm sure that God has something in store for you. Hang on to that thought. If it isn't clear now, it will be in the future."

I was grateful for his words, but they couldn't restore my sight or remove the agonizing anxiety I felt about Mary and our two teenagers. How was I to pick up the pieces and get our lives going again?

For a year I was in and out of hospitals, and my disillusionment about God kept swelling. Whenever home, I was fiercely determined to do everything I did before. I kept going to church, but more out of habit than conviction. It shocked and shamed me to find that I had no privacy; I couldn't even read my mail.

Right-handed, I now had to use my left to button a shirt or put on a sock, which was so frustrating I often ended up ripping the shirt apart. And the growing sense of alienation I felt toward the world grew worse when the visits and calls from fellow officers stopped. It made me miserable, but I understood it. My broken body reminded them how vulnerable they were.

But I did learn to dress myself, to write in a straight line, to walk, trust a cane, even to cook.

One night, trying to make conversation with Mary, Tony, and his wife, Carole, I exploded in self-pity, "Is this all that's left? Learning to dress myself? to fry an egg? Waiting for a phone call? Remembering what I was? Is this what God wants me to do for the rest of my life?"

At that moment Mary said something I had never heard her say before. "You're not the only one who is hurt," she said softly. "Carole and I hurt, too. Not like you and Tony, but we hurt."

"And there are other cops who hurt like you and Tony," Carole said. "You are not unique."

Their words churned in my head through a sleepless night. They were right. I was considering only myself, inflicting my torment on my family, my friends. And what about all the other injured police officers that Carole mentioned?

Next morning I wrote to a dozen top police officials, asking for a list of officers severely injured in the line of duty. An idea was growing inside my head. Maybe if we all got together, we could find ways to prove that we were not ready for the human junk pile, that we could be useful to one another. All the brass, including the commissioner, replied, listing a dozen names and offering a place where we could meet.

At our first meeting we quickly became aware that while we could not easily talk to others about our pain and problems, we could talk to one another. Alone we could not overcome our fears and confusions, but together we could. Gradually the men in that group began to reveal their desperate need for strength from God and understanding from men. We had all been to the same Calvary.

We call ourselves The Police Self-Support Groups. Those who could get around began visiting policemen recently hurt on duty. One of our men was Don Rios. He had been shot in the spine and was in a wheelchair. He had been told he could never have children. He was coming apart. So was his marriage. We got Don and his wife to a marriage counselor. Don manages to walk now. He and his wife are going to have their first child. And nowadays he is a regular visitor to injured policemen.

Some of us lost the services of doctors and therapists because department regulations required five months to pay medical bills. We cut it down to one month. One officer, who had been turned into a paraplegic by a bank robber's bullets, found it extremely difficult to travel. We persuaded doctors that the tests he needed could be done in one hospital, not two.

We meet once a month, but I keep busy six and seven days a week, softening family quarrels, helping wives face the realities of life with a permanently disabled husband, arranging psychological treatment for children who are afraid that the drug pushers who shot their fathers will return to kill them.

It's an age-old remedy for self-pity, I guess—getting out of yourself, doing for others—and gradually I found that as I went to church, I went, not out of habit, but because I wanted to worship God. No, the Lord did not abandon me. It's as if he was telling me, *I have other work for you now, work that requires a deep understanding of suffering*.

By leading me to help others, he is helping me. By restoring my faith, he healed me. I believe that fervently.

"Thank you, dear Lord, for giving me the blessing of your strength to meet the challenges of the day." That is the prayer that I once again say to him, every day.